Overcoming Materialism

Overcoming Materialism

by
John MacArthur, Jr.

MOODY PRESS
CHICAGO

Contents

CHAPTER

PAGE

1. Treasure in Heaven—Part 1
   Tape GC 2245—Matt. 6:19*a*

   1

2. Treasure in Heaven—Part 2
   Tape GC 2246—Matt. 6:19-24

   22

3. Mastery of Materialism
   Tape GC 2247—Selected Scriptures

   43

4. Overcoming Financial Worry—Part 1
   Tape GC 2248—Matt. 6:25-30*a*

   60

5. Overcoming Financial Worry—Part 2
   Tape GC 2249—Matt. 6:25-34

   80

Scripture Index

100

These Bible studies are taken from messages delivered by Pastor-Teacher John MacArthur, Jr., at Grace Community Church in Panorama City, California. The recorded messages themselves may be purchased as a series or individually. Please request the current price list by writing to:

WORD OF GRACE COMMUNICATIONS
P.O. Box 4000
Panorama City, CA 91412

Or call the following toll-free number:
1-800-55-GRACE

1
Treasure in Heaven— Part 1

Outline

Introduction
A. The Society of Things
   1. Consuming the things
   2. Corrupting the things
B. The Summary of the Sermon
   1. The right view of themselves
   2. The right view of the world
   3. The right view of the Word of God
   4. The right view of moral issues
   5. The right view of religious issues
   6. The right view of wealth and necessities
C. The System of Greed
   1. The false religion
      a) The Old Testament example
      b) The New Testament example
   2. The false concept
      a) The promise to Israel
         (1) The sign of obedience
         (2) The sign of disobedience
      b) The parade of spirituality
         (1) The wrong worship
         (2) The right warning

Lesson
I. Two Treasuries
A. The Principle
   1. Earthly treasures
      a) The reserve of wealth
         (1) Stacking
         (2) Stashing
      b) The right of ownership

      (1) The natural provision
      (2) The notable participants
      (3) The necessary Proverbs
      (4) The new plans
  c) The response of the heart
      (1) An investment in the kingdom
      (2) An investment in self
      (3) An investment in the church
      (4) An investment in the market
      (5) An investment in a principle
      (6) An investment in eternity

Introduction

Matthew 6:19-24 is the setting for these lessons: "Lay not up for yourselves treasures upon earth, where moth and rust doth corrupt, and where thieves break through and steal, but lay up for yourselves treasures in heaven, where neither moth nor rust doth corrupt, and where thieves do not break through nor steal; for where your treasure is, there will your heart be also. The lamp of the body is the eye; if, therefore, thine eye be healthy, thy whole body shall be full of light. But if thine eye be evil, thy whole body shall be full of darkness. If, therefore, the light that is in thee be darkness, how great is that darkness! No man can serve two masters; for either he will hate the one, and love the other; or else he will hold to the one, and despise the other. Ye cannot serve God and money."

A. The Society of Things

The question that arises out of this text is very simple: Where is your heart? According to verse 21, your heart is wherever your treasure is. Now, when I say, "Where is your heart?" I am not talking about the heart's physiological location; I am not talking about the person you are hopelessly in love with and have given your heart to; but I am talking in terms of the investment of your life, motives, attitudes, and thought patterns. Where is the concentration and the preoccupation of your life? What particular object do you spend most of your thinking, planning, and energy on? Chances are, you are like most people and spend your time thinking about some thing (a house, a car, a wardrobe, a bank account, a savings account, a bond, a stock, an investment, furniture, and so on). We are creatures committed to things—that is part of the curse on the society in which we live. Some societies are too poor to have things. But we are a society of things.

2

1. Consuming the things

   Listen to this analysis: "Mr. and Mrs. Thing are a very pleasant and successful couple. At least, that's the verdict of most people, who tend to measure success with a 'thingometer.' And when the 'thingometer' is put to work in the life of Mr. and Mrs. Thing, the result is startling.

   "There he is, sitting down on a luxurious and very expensive thing, almost hidden by the large number of [other] things. . . . Things to sit on, things to sit at, things to cook on, things to eat from, all shining and new. Things, things, things.

   "Things to clean with, things to wash with, things to clean, and things to wash. Things to amuse, things to give pleasure, things to watch, and things to play. Things for the long, hot summers, things for the short, cold winters. Things for the big thing in which they live, things for the garden, things for the lounge, things for the kitchen, and things for the bedroom. Things on four wheels, things on two wheels, things to put on top of the four wheels, things to pull behind the four wheels, things to add to the interior of the thing on four wheels. . . .

   "Well, Mr. Thing, I've some bad news for you. What's that? You can't hear me? The things are in the way? . . . But then, that's the problem with things. Look at that thing standing outside your house. Whatever its value to the secondhand thingdealer, it means a lot to you. But then, an error in judgment, a temporary loss of concentration, and that thing can be a mass of mangled metal being towed off to the junkyard.*

   That's the way life goes. In spite of how stupid it sounds, we are basically committed to acquiring things.

2. Corrupting the things

   Sadly, the leading religionists of Jesus' day had the same problem. They were totally consumed with things. This must also be included among all of the other problems of the Pharisees: they were thing-oriented, greedy, avaricious, covetous, manipulative, and they moved toward grasping more things. As we approach this element of the Sermon on the Mount in Matthew 6:19-24, Jesus

   *Source unknown.

directs some statements to the Pharisees who were abusing this whole matter of possessions.

B. The Summary of the Sermon

The thrust of the Sermon on the Mount (Matt. 5-7) is to sweep aside the low, inadequate, insufficient standard of the Pharisees and reaffirm God's divine standard for life in His kingdom. They had invented a system of religion that was substandard, man-made, inadequate, inefficient, and ineffective. The key to the sermon is in Matthew 5:20*b*, where the Lord says, "Except your righteousness shall exceed the righteousness of the scribes and Pharisees, ye shall in no case enter into the kingdom of heaven." In other words, "To be in My kingdom you must live up to this standard." So, He affirmed the standard in contrast to the Pharisees.

1. The right view of themselves

For example, in Matthew 5:1-12 He says, "To be in My kingdom you must have the right view of yourself." The Pharisees were proud, egocentric, and self-sufficient. But you need to be broken in spirit, mourning over sin, meek, and hungering and thirsting after righteousness.

2. The right view of the world

You must also have the right relationship to the world (Matt. 5:13-16). The Pharisees were part of the corruption and the darkness, but you must be salt to retard the corruption and light to dispel the darkness.

3. The right view of the Word of God

You must not only have the right view of yourself and the right view of the world, but you must have the right view of the Word of God (Matt. 5:17-20). The Pharisees had developed their own system, but you must be committed to the Word of God, and not one jot or tittle shall pass from that law until it is all fulfilled.

4. The right view of moral issues

You must have the right view of moral issues (Matt. 5:21-48). The Pharisees were concerned only with the externals: don't kill, don't commit adultery, and so on. Moral issues are not just what you do or don't do, they are what you think or don't think.

5. The right view of religious issues

Then in Matthew 6:1-18 He says, "You must have the

right view of religious issues." The Pharisees were fasting, praying, and giving, but it was all hypocritical. You must fast, give, and pray, but with a right motive. In other words, the sermon is set in contrast to the system of religion of the day dominated by the thinking of the Pharisees and the scribes. Jesus was saying that God's standard exceeded their standard, and it is adherence to His standard that is required for being in His kingdom.

6. The right view of wealth and necessities

Now, in Matthew 6:19-34 He says, "You must also have the right view of wealth and luxury [vv. 19-24], then you must have the right view of necessities" (vv. 25-34). First, He deals with the wealth that we have and then with our necessity to eat, sleep, have a place to stay, and have some clothing to wear. In both cases the Pharisees had the wrong perspective. So, in every element of Christ's message, He sets Himself and His Word in contrast to the Pharisees: "Your view of wealth and luxury must exceed that of the scribes and Pharisees if you want to be a part of My kingdom. They have the wrong perspective. They are laying up for themselves treasures on earth—consumed with greed and covetousness. That is not the standard."

So verses 19-24 deal with how we view our luxuries and our wealth. We live in a society where all of us need to learn to deal with this because all of us are wealthy in comparison to the rest of the world. Our text shows us how to handle those luxuries and possessions of ours that are beyond the simple necessities of eating, drinking, sleeping, and clothing. If we are in His kingdom, we must face what He says.

C. The System of Greed

1. The false religion

Matthew 6:1-18 shows the hypocrisy of the Pharisees' religion, and it follows that wherever you have hypocritical religion you will have greed. So our Lord deals with their view of wealth and money. Wherever you find a false teacher, invariably you will find that he is in it for the money. That is why the Bible says that we are not to discharge our ministry for the sake of filthy lucre (1 Pet. 5:2). The Bible characterizes hypocritical religion in two ways: it is greedy of money, and it is immoral in its lusts.

5

Those two things follow in the course of false religions and false religious leaders.

a) The Old Testament example

Even in the Old Testament this was true. Where there was hypocrisy, there was greed for money. For example, in 1 Samuel 2, Eli is the high priest in Israel—the key religious leader. He had two sons named Hophni and Phinehas. They were men of great responsibility—sons of the high priest and responsible before God and the people. But they were phonies and absolute hypocrites. They were totally immoral, lustful, lascivious, and lewd, living a pornographic type of life on the very steps of the place where God was worshiped. They were evil, vile men, whom the Lord finally struck dead.

Since Hophni and Phinehas were spiritual phonies, they were characterized by greed. This is illustrated in 1 Samuel 2. According to Leviticus 7, a portion of the offering that was brought to the Lord goes to the priest (i.e., the breast and the right shoulder; Lev. 7:30-35). But Hophni and Phinehas said, "When the offerings come, we will examine them and take what we want and leave the residue for the Lord." They were in it to get what they could. When people brought their offering to the Lord, they demanded to see the offering first and then selected what they wanted for their own indulgence. Whatever was left went to the Lord (1 Sam. 2:12-16). They were covetous and greedy. First Samuel 2:17 says, "Wherefore the sin of the young men was very great before the Lord; for men abhorred the offering of the Lord." They were tampering with things that belonged to God.

b) The New Testament example

The Pharisees were doing the same thing—using their religious position to fill their pockets. Twice Jesus had to take a whip and cleanse the Temple (Matt. 21:12-13; John 2:13-17). They were using their religious position to get rich. There is nothing more foul smelling to the nostrils of God than hypocrisy and greed. I daresay there are people in our own country who are doing exactly the same thing. Wherever there is religious hypocrisy, inevitably there is the problem of greed.

2. The false concept

To the Pharisees, being rich was a sign of holiness. In other words, "I'm rich because I'm so righteous that God is blessing me." When the Lord said, "It is easier for a camel to go through the eye of a needle, than for a rich man to enter into the kingdom of God" (Matt. 19:24), that was absolutely and utterly shocking. To the Pharisees, riches were the stamp of divine approval on one's life because God gave riches to those who were righteous. To say that a rich man could no more enter the kingdom than a camel could go through the eye of a needle was really a shocking statement because they equated money with the blessing of God. So they greedily gathered money, and the richer they became the more they pretended to the people that they were spiritual. Annas and Caiaphas ran concessions in the Temple that made them extremely wealthy men along with everyone who could cash in on the deal.

a) The promise to Israel

Where did they get this concept? They may have first developed the concept from Deuteronomy 28. When the Lord delivered Israel from Egypt and brought them to the edge of Canaan (i.e., the Promised Land, the land of milk and honey, the land that God had promised to give them), He laid down some conditions for their entrance into the land. And on the basis of those conditions being met, He laid down some wonderful promises.

(1) The sign of obedience

As they are preparing to go into the land, the Lord says in Deuteronomy 28:1-2, "And it shall come to pass, if thou shalt hearken diligently unto the voice of the Lord thy God, to observe and to do all his commandments which I command thee this day, that the Lord thy God will set thee on high above all nations of the earth; and all these blessings shall come on thee, and overtake thee, if thou shalt hearken unto the voice of the Lord thy God." The basic command regards

7

obedience: "If you do what I say, I will bless you."

How will the blessings come? Verses 3-6 say, "Blessed shalt thou be in the city, and blessed shalt thou be in the field. Blessed shall be the fruit of thy body [your children], and the fruit of thy ground [your crops], and the fruit of thy cattle, the increase of thy cows, and the flocks of thy sheep. Blessed shall be thy basket and thy kneading-trough. Blessed shalt thou be when thou comest in, and blessed shalt thou be when thou goest out." Notice that all the blessings were material—physical, tangible, visible, earthly blessings.

(2) The sign of disobedience

Conversely, verses 15-19 say, "But it shall come to pass, if thou wilt not hearken unto the voice of the Lord thy God, to observe to do all his commandments and his statutes which I command thee this day, that all these curses shall come upon thee, and overtake thee. Cursed shalt thou be in the city, and cursed shalt thou be in the field. Cursed shall be thy basket and thy kneading-trough. Cursed shall be the fruit of thy body, and the fruit of thy land, the increase of thy cows, and the flocks of thy sheep. Cursed shalt thou be when thou comest in, and cursed shalt thou be when thou goest out." In other words, "Material blessing is a sign of your obedience; material poverty is a sign of your disobedience."

b) The parade of spirituality

(1) The wrong worship

I believe the Pharisees had probably begun to build their phony system from things like this: "The more you have, the more it proves that God is blessing you." That is a misinterpretation of Deuteronomy 28. The acquisition of material wealth became their greatest goal, in order that they could parade their phony righteousness and say, "Look what God has done for me. See how holy I am." They may have even misapplied

Proverbs 10:22*a*, which says, "The blessing of the Lord, it maketh rich." They desperately wanted money and became perverted, greedy, and

(2) The right warning

The Old Testament warned against this:

(*a*) Solomon was rich and yet it was "vanity of vanities; all is vanity" (Eccles. 1:2*b*).

(*b*) In the Decalogue, Exodus 20:17*a*, God says "Thou shalt not covet." The Old Testament is replete with warnings against seeking riches.

(*c*) Proverbs 23:4*a* says, "Labor not to be rich."

(*d*) Proverbs 28:20*b* says, "He that maketh haste to be rich shall not be innocent." In other words, the Bible warns against greed, covetousness, hastiness, and being rich.

But in spite of all of these warnings, Luke 16:14 says that the Pharisees were covetous. They wanted money, material wealth, and possessions. They were earthly because their religion was false. Our Lord spoke against the backdrop of the greed of the Pharisees. He said that we must have the proper view of money, wealth, and possessions. We must handle our possessions, our money, our wealth, and our luxury as we do anything else. First Corinthians 10:31 says, "Whether, therefore, ye eat, or drink, or whatever ye do, do all to the glory of God." But our problem is that we do so much of it to the indulgence of self.

In order to know how to handle our luxuries, we are given three alternatives in this text. There are two treasuries, two visions, and two masters. In each of these three the same principle is approached from a different angle and then followed by some subordinate reasons for obeying that principle. First, we have to make a choice whether to lay up our treasure on earth or in heaven (vv. 19-21). Second, we make a choice whether to exist in light or darkness (vv. 22-23). Finally, we make a choice of masters—will it be God or will it be money? The master cannot be both. The three choices the Lord gives are really one: How should we handle our wealth? This is a difficult choice to make. As John Stott has said, "Worldly ambition has a strong fascination for us.

The spell of materialism is hard to break." He is right—it is difficult.

Will you let God change your attitude?

It would be so easy if the Lord would just say, "In order to solve this problem, just take fifty percent of everything you own and give it to Me." Wouldn't that be easy? We could all say, "I gave my fifty percent; did you give yours?" We could discipline them right out of the church if they didn't because we would have a standard—cut and dried, absolute, formulated, tabulated, learned by rote, and cranked out. But the problem with that is we would never get to the real issue—the heart attitude. God does not want to receive something that is given because we are afraid of Him; He wants to receive something that is given because we love Him. The Lord does not give us an absolute, legalistic standard; He merely gives us a principle. It is not just some external formula but a principle that will deal with our attitude. Be ready to let God change your attitude.

Lesson

I. TWO TREASURIES (vv. 19-21)

A. The Principle (vv. 19*a*, 20*a*)

"Lay not up for yourselves treasures upon earth . . . but lay up for yourselves treasures in heaven."

You have an option to choose between two treasuries—one on earth, one in heaven. Jesus said, "Put it in heaven, not on earth." What do you do with your wealth? Don't invest it here; invest it there, "for where your treasure is, there will your heart be also" (v. 21).

The Root of Evil

The apostle Paul said to Timothy, "For the love of money is the root of all evil" (1 Tim. 6:10*a*). The money is not the root of all evil; the love of it is. You can have no money and still love it madly. It is the love of money that corrupts.

1. Achan (Josh. 7)

Instead of inheriting the Promised Land, he died with his entire family because he decided to take what God forbade. Due to his love of money, when he saw a beautiful garment and some coins, he stashed them in the ground in his tent. The Lord confronted him through Joshua, who said, "You had better confess your sin because you're going to die." He did, and he and his entire family died.

2. Solomon (Eccles. 1:2)

   He kept amassing fortunes until he was the wealthiest man in the world. When he reached that position he said, "Vanity of vanities; all is vanity" (v. 2b). It was all empty, useless, meaningless, and void.

3. Ananias and Sapphira (Acts 5:1-11)

   They decided to keep some of the money while implying they were giving it all to the Lord, but God struck them dead.

4. Judas (Matt. 27:5; Acts 1:18-19)

   For a pittance he sold the Son of God and went out and hanged himself. His body burst open and his bowels gushed forth as he crashed to the rocks below.

5. Demas (2 Tim. 4:10)

   Paul said of him, "He has forsaken me because he loved the system."

There are many illustrations of people who were devastated and destroyed to some degree because of the love of money. We all need to learn this because it is destructive to ourselves and those around us.

1. Earthly treasures (v. 19a)

   "Lay not up for yourselves treasures upon earth."

   a) The reserve of wealth

      (1) Stacking

          Let me give you a word study on "treasures." The Greek word is *thēsaurizete*, from which we get the word *thesaurus*—a treasury of words. But *thēsaurizete* is a play on words that means "treasure not up treasures." In other words, don't stockpile. The idea of the word *treasure* is to stash something somewhere. The peculiar quality of this Greek word literally conveys the idea of placing something horizontally.

          You may remember this old adage: "The miser

says coins are flat that they may rest in stacks; the spendthrift says they are round that they may roll." We are discussing the miser. There is a horizontal concept in the word *thēsaurizete*. When something is stacked it is not being used—it is in a passive condition. When you find a word in the Greek that has a vertical or perpendicular flavor, it means that it is in active use—purposeful, meaningful, with a function, being invested in some purpose, goal, or end. But the meaning here is something flat, stacked with no active function or purpose.

(2) Stashing

The Lord is not referring to that which we use to live every day, but that which we just pile up. It is not our necessities (i.e., meeting the needs of our own lives, families, the poor, the Lord, setting aside money for the future, or making wise investments in order to be better stewards of God's money in the days to come). It is not active but stockpiled luxury we amass for our selves and beyond what we can possibly use. The implication is that there is an abundance too great for use, so it is just piled up.

b) The right of ownership

What was Jesus forbidding? Was He forbidding a bank account, savings account, life insurance policy, or a wise investment? Does He mean that we shouldn't possess anything when He says, "Lay not up for yourselves treasures upon earth" (v. 19a)? Some people say, "That means you shouldn't possess anything—don't have any earthly treasure." In other words, sell all you own, walk the street, get a brown bag, and be a hobo. They also say, "What about the rich young ruler? Jesus said to him, 'Sell all you own and give it to the poor'" (Matt. 19:21). But notice that he is the only one Jesus ever said this to. He never said this to Mary or Martha. He also said, "And every one that hath forsaken houses, or brethren, or sisters, or father, or mother, or wife, or children, or lands, for my name's sake, shall receive an hundredfold" (Matt. 19:29). The Lord never condemns possessions. He told the rich young ruler to sell all he owned because

12

it stood between him and God. Until he got rid of it, he could not have a relationship with God.

(1) The natural provision

(a) Deuteronomy 28:1-14—God said to Israel, "I'll put you in the land, and I'll prosper your families, cattle, sheep, and crops." The Lord is not saying we shouldn't possess anything.

(b) Exodus 20:15—"Thou shalt not steal." That very statement of God in the Decalogue assumes that something can be mine that you can't have. We have a right to possessions. The Bible tells men not to steal or rob because people have a right to their possessions. You not only have no right to steal what is mine, but you don't even have a right to want what is mine.

(c) Exodus 20:17a—"Thou shalt not covet." The Lord recognizes the right to ownership of goods and personal property.

(d) Acts 5:1-11—Ananias and Sapphira owned a piece of property. They said, "Let's sell the property and give all the money to the Lord." They made a big announcement: "We're going to sell our property and give all the money to the Lord." The Bible didn't tell them to do that and neither did God; they wanted to do it voluntarily. So they sold the property, and when they saw all the money they said, "Let's keep some of the money." As a result, the Lord knocked them dead in front of the entire church. But before He killed them He gave them a message through Peter: "Ananias, why hath Satan filled thine heart to lie to the Holy Spirit, and to keep back part of the price of the land? While it remained, was it not thine own? And after it was sold, was it not in thine own power?" (Acts 5:3b-4a). In other words, "It was yours, you had power over it, you had control over it, you didn't have to sell it, and you didn't have to promise it. But the issue is that you lied to God." Even so, the point is that it was their land, and once they had given it in a

13

promise, they needed to follow through. The Lord has given us the right to possess things. All He wants is to be sure that our attitude is right in the manner in which we possess them.

(e) Deuteronomy 8:18b—"For it is he who giveth thee power to get wealth." God has given us the power, the resources, and the abilities to get wealth.

(f) 1 Corinthians 4:7b—"And what hast thou that thou didst not receive?" The implication is that it is from God.

(g) 1 Timothy 6:17b—"God, who giveth us richly all things to enjoy." We don't have to live a monastic life. For my birthday my wife bought me a chair—a nice soft chair that reclines. I can sit in that chair and not have to think that I'm carnal because I own a chair. I can enjoy that chair. God has given us richly all thing to enjoy. He is not withholding from us. God is a God of great generosity.

(2) The notable participants

(a) Business and wise banking principles are encouraged by our Lord in His parables in Matthew 25 and Luke 19.

(b) The very rich man Abraham was called a friend of God (2 Chron. 20:7).

(c) God made Job wealthier than he had been before he lost everything. And he was so wealthy before that he couldn't count it all (Job 42:12).

(d) Zaccheus was rich and yet was counted a son of Abraham (Luke 19:2, 9).

(3) The necessary Proverbs

The book of Proverbs encourages us to be careful how we handle our funds so that we will make wise investments.

(a) Proverbs 6:6a, 8—"Go to the ant . . . consider her ways . . . [she] provideth her food in the summer, and gathereth her food

14

in the harvest." An ant is smart enough to plan for the future and to make wise savings.

(b) Proverbs 14:23—"In all labor there is profit; but the talk of the lips tendeth only to penury." In other words, if you want to be rich, work; if you want to be poor, talk.

(c) Proverbs 21:20—"There is a treasure to be desired, and oil, in the dwelling of the wise, but a foolish man spendeth it up." In other words, a wise man knows how to save and how to plan.

(d) Proverbs 22:7b—"The borrower is servant to the lender." It is wiser to have to lend than to have to borrow.

(e) Proverbs 24:3-4—"Through wisdom is an house builded, and by understanding it is established; and by knowledge shall the chambers be filled with all precious and pleasant riches." A wise person knows how to build a house and fill it with pleasant and precious treasures. God is not against that. He has given us graciously these wonderful things to enjoy.

(f) Proverbs 28:19—"He that tilleth his land shall have plenty of bread, but he that followeth after vain persons shall have poverty enough." In other words, you are better off to work your ground than to chase wildcat schemes. You have a right to possess and to enrich those possessions.

So Scripture tells us that not laying up treasure on earth is not a prohibition against possessing, enjoying, or accepting from God's good hand those abundant things He's given us.

(4) The new plans

The New Testament says the same thing:

(a) Romans 12:11a—"[Be] not slothful in business."

(b) 2 Corinthians 12:14—Parents should plan wisely so they can take care of their children in the future.

(c)   1 Timothy 5:8—We are to plan to take care of our own and to provide for our household or we are worse than an infidel. In other words, God is saying these things are ours by His grace.

c)   The response of the heart

Now, what is Jesus forbidding when He says, "Lay not up for yourselves treasures upon earth" (v. 19a)? He is not talking about what we have; He is talking about the attitude toward what we have. It is right to provide for my family, it is right to plan for the future, it is right to make wise investments, it is right to help the poor, it is right to have enough money to carry on my business. But it is wrong to be greedy and covetous. Again, the motive is the issue. If I am using my possessions to the glory of God in the lives of those around me and for His kingdom, then I have a right to all of it. But if I am gaining it to stockpile, hoard, keep and amass in order to indulge myself— that is sin.

(1)   An investment in the kingdom

John Wesley was an extremely wealthy man. We think of John Wesley as a great man of God, of prayer, and devoted to time in the Word of God. He was up every morning for hours studying in the Greek text. We think of him as a man of low means, but John Wesley was extremely wealthy. He gained his wealth from the hymns he wrote and the books he penned. At one point in his life he gave away 40,000 pounds sterling—a fortune in his time. Yet, when John Wesley died his estate was worth 28 pounds. He didn't lay up his treasure on earth. When it came in it went right back out into the lives of the people—invested in the kingdom of God. The issue is that we don't pile up what we don't need and don't plan to use. Some people stockpile under the guise that they are hedging against some coming doom. The problem with that is you don't live by faith—you don't believe God will take care of you in the future.

16

(2) An investment in self

A certain professor at the University of Southern California saved $1,000 to invest in a piece of real estate. It was a good investment. So he made another and another and another. He eventually stopped teaching because he was worth hundreds of millions of dollars. He recently made a $68 million purchase. He is an incredibly wealthy man, but he looks fifteen years beyond his age, and he has lost his family in the process. He has millions piled up all around him. For what? Then I think about the work of God that continues on a shoestring budget, struggling and stretching for everything. Are we giving all we can give, or are we just possessive?

(3) An investment in the church

One man I know who sets the right example is Dr. W. A. Criswell of the First Baptist Church of Dallas. Some people have criticized him because he is wealthy. When he was younger he had made some very good investments. One day, after thirty years as a pastor of the church, he presented a check to the church as a gift. It was written for the amount of every penny they had ever paid him in thirty years, plus interest. Someone asked one of the church staff members if he received a salary. He said, "Yes, but he gives more every year than he receives."

The issue is not what you have but what you do with what you have. Is it for you or for the kingdom of God and His purposes? Someone has said, "There is no smaller package than a man wrapped up in himself." Colossians 3:5 says that covetousness is idolatry. That is what our Lord had in mind. Money can become your god.

(4) An investment in the market

A member of our church came to me one day and said, "John, I have a spiritual problem." I said, "What is it?" He said, "I have five hundred shares of stock in an oil company, and it is ruining my spiritual life. It is like idolatry to me. So I'm here to give it to you." I said, "I don't want your spiritual problems. I have my own." But he insisted, "I think it will be a good test of your spirituality. I'll watch how you handle it." So he gave me 500 shares of stock in this company. Do you know what that did to me? It messed up my mind. I would worry about that stock and watch it go up and down. Finally, I said to myself, "This is messing me up about as badly as it did him." So I sold it for 50¢ a share—$250. That was it. And I haven't even thought about it since then except for one day when someone said, "Do you still have your stock? It's worth ten dollars a share." I'm glad I didn't have it for all that time to worry about it.

The things that we possess can become the idols of our lives. The Lord is telling us to not horizontally pile up things. The selfish accumulation of goods is extravagant luxury and results in hardheartedness toward the cause of God.

(5) An investment in a principle

Here is the key to verse 19a: "Lay not up for yourselves." If I want to invest, or pursue a successful business, or be aggressive and honest in what I do, or do the best I can for others, for God, for my children, for my parents, for the poor, and for the depressed and the oppressed— that is one thing. But when I pile it up for myself in extravagant luxury and become materialistic, then I have violated the principle.

A rich man died. One of his acquaintances said to another, "What did he leave?" To which the friend replied, "All of it." An Old Testament saint in effect said, "Give me enough so I don't starve and doubt your faithfulness, but don't give me too much or I'll forget You" (Prov. 30:8-9).

(6) An investment in eternity

Examine your heart. Jesus is saying, "People in My kingdom don't amass fortunes or stockpile things for themselves." Do you live in contrast to the Pharisees, or do you have their problem? If you are focusing on money you may not even be a Christian, because people of Christ's kingdom are laying up treasure in heaven—investing in eternity. If you asked me if I would rather spend $5000 for a car or put $5000 into the life of a missionary, there would be no choice for me. I would rather see the eternal dividend. That choice is easy for me because I have to make it every day. When I examine my life and don't see the desire to invest in eternity and in God's causes, to be unselfish about it, and giving more and more to God's work and freely dispensing it with joy in my heart, then I should question the legitimacy of my claim to being a believer. It is characteristic of a believer that his treasure be in heaven. Examine your heart. Are you really a Christian?

Alistair Begg, a pastor from Scotland, tells the story of a little boy in a river, flailing his arms and splattering the water. On the shore immediately in front of the little boy is a sign, "No Swimming." A man walks up, looks into the water and says, "Laddie, you can no read the sign? No swimming." The boy said, "Please sir, I'm not swimming—I'm drowning!" Sometimes, swimming and drowning look alike. We think some people in the church are swimming when actually they are drowning. You need to examine your heart. What is your attitude toward luxury, wealth and money?

Focusing on the Facts

1. What was one of the main problems of the Pharisees that Jesus addresses in Matthew 6:19-24 (see p. 4)?
2. What was Jesus' main purpose in giving the Sermon on the Mount (see p. 4)?
3. What are the right views that Christians should maintain? Contrast these with the incorrect views of the Pharisees (see pp. 4-5).
4. What naturally follows hypocritical religion (see p. 5)?
5. Explain how Hophni and Phinehas manifested their hypocrisy (see p. 6).
6. What meaning did the possession of riches have for the Pharisees? Why (see p. 7)?
7. What was one possible source where the Pharisees could have obtained this particular concept of riches (see p. 7)?
8. What was the sign of obedience for the nation of Israel? What was the sign of their disobedience (see pp. 7-8)?

9. Explain how the Old Testament warns against the greed manifested by the Pharisees (see p. 9).
10. What three choices does Jesus offer in Matthew 6:19-24 (see p. 9)?
11. What are the two treasuries we have to choose from (see p. 10)?
12. What is the root of all evil? Give some examples to support your answer (see pp. 10-11).
13. What is Jesus attempting to convey when He uses the term "treasures"? Explain the difference between the horizontal concept and the vertical concept in the use of words (see p. 12).
14. Why can't you use the story of the rich ruler to show that the Lord doesn't want us to own anything (see pp. 12-13)?
15. How does Exodus 20:15 show that God has granted the right of ownership to individuals (see p. 13)?
16. Why did God kill Ananias and Sapphira? What was wrong about their attitude toward their possession (see pp. 13-14)?
17. What is Jesus forbidding in Matthew 6:19a (see p. 16)?
18. What makes John Wesley a good example of how the Lord wants us to handle our possessions (see p. 16)?
19. What are the key words in Matthew 6:19a? Why (see p. 18)?

Pondering the Principles

1. Where is your heart? Is the concentration and preoccupation of your life consumed with the things you own, or is it consumed with the things of God? Make a list of the different things you do during the week. Next to each item, make a notation indicating whether that time is spent for you or for God. How do you spend the majority of your time? Do you need to spend more of your time concentrating on heavenly things? Take one of the items from your list and determine to not spend that time on yourself. Instead, make it your priority this week to invest that time with God. Do this with another item from your list the following week until you are spending more of your available time on the things of the Lord.

2. To better internalize the priorities of your life, memorize 1 Corinthians 10:31: "Whether, therefore, ye eat, or drink, or whatever ye do, do all to the glory of God." As you memorize, examine your heart attitude. Do you desire to give God glory because you love Him or because you are afraid of Him? Remember, God wants you to give Him glory because you love Him.

3. Examine your life in terms of the things that God has given you. Do you selfishly accumulate things for yourself, or do you use what God has given you to bring Him glory by ministering to the needs of those around you? How do you respond when something in your possession is stolen? Do you react strongly against the person who stole it, or do you think of it as something that belongs to God and that it is His to do with as He wills? It is characteristic of a true believer that his treasure be in heaven. Take this time to examine your life before God. Does the location of your treasure manifest that you are indeed a believer, or does it manifest that you are just like others who belong to the world? Ask God to reveal your true heart to you. If changes are necessary in your life, ask God to help you to turn from your pride and humbly submit to His will. Remember, it is not a question of whether you can, but whether you will.

2

Treasure in Heaven—
Part 2

Outline

Introduction
A. The Location of the Heart
    1.   The illustration
    2.   The issue
        a) External code
        b) Internal code
B. The Giving of the Heart
    1.   An appropriate response
        a) The revival initiated
        b) The result identified
        c) The response imparted
    2.   An attached heart

Review
I. Two Treasuries
  A. The Principle
    1.   Earthly treasures

Lesson
    2.   Heavenly treasures
        a) Storing the riches
           (1) The commitment of King Monobaz
           (2) The commitment of the early church
               (*a*) During Pentecost
               (*b*) During the Decian persecution
        b) Securing the dividends
           (1) Proverbs 3:9-10
           (2) Proverbs 11:24-25*a*
           (3) 2 Corinthians 9:6
           (4) Luke 6:38
        c) Seeking the reward

                    (1) The general reward
                    (2) The specific reward
                         (*a*) 1 Timothy 6:17-19
                         (*b*) Luke 12:33*a*
                         (*c*) Luke 16:9
                         (*d*) Proverbs 19:17
     B. The Reasons
          1. The earthly problems
               a) Garments
                    (1) The possession of garments
                         (*a*) Gehazi
                         (*b*) Achan
                         (*c*) Joseph
                         (*d*) Samson
                    (2) The problem with garments
               b) Grain
               c) Gold
          2. The heavenly perspective
II. Two Visions
     A. The Explanation
          1. The principle
          2. The reasons
               a) The single eye
                    (1) The meaning
                         (*a*) James 1:5*b*
                         (*b*) Romans 12:8
                         (*c*) 2 Corinthians 9:13
                    (2) The misappropriation
               b) The evil eye
                    (1) Proverbs 23:6*a*
                    (2) Proverbs 28:22
     B. The Exclamation
III. Two Masters
     A. The Principle
     B. The Reasons
          1. Required responsibilities
               a) Exclusive devotion
               b) Eliminating division
          2. Opposite orders
               a) Bishop Ryle
               b) Caleb
               c) David

Introduction

D. Martyn Lloyd-Jones tells the story of a farmer who one day went happily and with great joy in his heart to report to his wife and family that their best cow had given birth to twin calves, one brown and one white. And he said, "You know I suddenly had a feeling and impulse that we must dedicate one of these calves to the Lord. We will bring them up together, and when the time comes we will sell one and keep the proceeds, and we will sell the other and give the proceeds to the Lord's work." His wife asked him which he was going to dedicate to the Lord. "There is no need to bother about that now," he replied. "We will treat them both in the same way, and when the time comes we will do as I say." And off he went. In a few months the man entered his kitchen looking very miserable and unhappy. When his wife asked him what was troubling him, he answered, "I have bad news to give you. The Lord's calf is dead."

Why is it always the Lord's calf that dies? We laugh at that because we all tend to lay up treasure on earth. The pull of the sin that is in us is like a magnet dragging us down to the earth. We want to be rich toward self and poor toward God. Jesus speaks directly to this perspective on life in Matthew 6:19-24. He gives us tremendous insight into how we should really view the matter of wealth, money, and luxuries. In the following passage, from verses 25 to 34, He talks about necessities—eating, drinking, clothing, and a place to sleep—the bare necessities and how we should deal with them. But in this portion He is discussing luxury, not necessity.

A. The Location of the Heart

   We are confronted with a significant statement in Matthew 6:19a: "Lay not up for yourselves treasures upon earth," and a corresponding one in verse 20a: "But lay up for yourselves treasures in heaven." The heart of the matter is in verse 21: "For where your treasure is, there will your heart be also." Ask yourself this question in regard to your life: Is it always the Lord's cow that dies? When you have to decide if something is for you or for Him, whom is it usually for? That is the real issue. Where is your heart? It is where your treasure is. Wherever you put your investment is where you will put your heart. If all that you possess is locked up in commodities, accounts, notes, and savings, that is where your heart is going to be. But if it is in the process of being invested in God's causes, then that is where your heart is going to be.

   1.   The illustration

Many missionaries have come across my path. I am not always as sensitive to their needs as I ought to be, but on one occasion I recognized the need of a certain missionary for a suit of clothes. One day I took him to a store to buy him a suit. I said, "I would like to give you whatever kind of suit you want, as a gift." So he picked out a suit. There are many missionaries that I have met and forgotten, but not that one because I made an investment in his life. Where my treasure is, my heart tends to be. As a result, I have thought of and prayed for him often.

2. The issue

Where I set my heart is really the critical issue in my spiritual life. It will determine how I perceive everything. If my heart is right and my treasure is in heaven, then I am going to have the right kind of spiritual perception. My treasure will be where my heart is because I have to attach myself to my investment.

a) External code

Now, the Pharisees' hearts were in the earth. They were phonies—their morality was totally external, and their humility was nonexistent. Instead of being salt and light, they were part of the corruption and the darkness. Instead of believing in the law of God, they defied it and substituted their own tradition. Instead of having an internal set of principles, they had nothing but an external code of semispiritual ethics. Instead of having genuine worship, they had a false standard of pure hypocrisy. Everything about them was external, self-centered, and self-motivated.

b) Internal code

In contrast to the Pharisees, the Lord is saying, "You must have a right heart." The key verse in the Sermon on the Mount is Matthew 5:20b: "Your righteousness shall exceed the righteousness of the scribes and Pharisees." They had an external righteousness without a right heart. Your heart and your treasure go together—they both need to be in heaven. Our Lord is speaking of a single-minded devotion to God and His causes that is undistracted by the world.

25

B. The Giving of the Heart

I believe that when your heart is right, your giving will be right. When the heart is right, the treasure follows after the heart.

1. An appropriate response

Nehemiah was God's man to rebuild the fallen walls of Jerusalem after the Babylonian captivity. Using the people of the land, he rebuilt the wall in fifty-two days. When the wall was completed, a great event took place—a revival.

a) The revival initiated

The revival was initiated in Nehemiah 8:1 when Ezra brought the book of the law of Moses. Revival always begins with the bringing of the Book—the Word of God. Verse 5 begins, "And Ezra opened the book in the sight of all the people (for he was above all the people); and when he opened it, all the people stood up. And Ezra blessed the Lord, the great God. And all the people answered, Amen, Amen, lifting up their hands; and they bowed their heads, and worshiped the Lord with their faces to the ground. . . . So they read in the book in the law of God distinctly, and gave the sense, and caused them to understand the reading" (vv. 5-6, 8). They read the law of God, and it generated a heart response.

b) The result identified

Nehemiah 9 records that four things came as a result of the reading of the law. One, conviction of sin—they began to confess their sin; two, a desire for obedience; three, praise; and four, a covenant, or promise. First they were convicted of their sin. Then they began to praise God and to express a desire to obey God. Then they affirmed that they wanted to make a promise, or a covenant. Nehemiah 9:38 says, "And because of all this we make a sure covenant, and write it; and our princes, Levites, and priests, set their seal to it." In the sight of all their spiritual leaders they wanted to make a vow to God—a covenant, or promise—as a result of their hearts being revived through the reading of the Word. What does a revival produce? It will produce conviction of sin, a desire for obedience, praise, and a covenant. In

26

other words, a decision to start walking in a new direction.

c) The response imparted

What was their covenant? Nehemiah 10:32 says, "Also we made ordinances for us, to charge ourselves yearly with the third part of a shekel for the service of the house of our God." The first thing they wanted to affirm, other than general obedience to the law of God, was the payment of the required third-of-a-shekel Temple tax. Verse 33 says, "For the showbread, and for the continual meal offering, and for the continual burnt offering, of the sabbaths, of the new moons, for the set feasts, and for the holy things, and for the sin offerings to make an atonement for Israel, and for all the work of the house of our God." In other words, they would give to support the functioning of the house of God. The point is this: when the heart is made right, the initial response is giving.

Further, verses 35-39a say, "And to bring the first fruits of our ground, and the first fruits of all fruit of all trees, year by year, unto the house of the Lord: also the first-born of our sons, and of our cattle, as it is written in the law, and the firstlings of our herds and of our flocks, to bring to the house of our God, unto the priests who minister in the house of our God; and that we should bring the first fruits of our dough, and our offerings, and the fruit of all manner of trees, of wine and of oil, unto the priests, to the chambers of the house of our God; and the tithes of our ground unto the Levites, that the same Levites might have the tithes in all the cities of our tillage. And the priest, the son of Aaron, shall be with the Levites, when the Levites take tithes; and the Levites shall bring up the tithe of the tithes unto the house of our God, to the chambers, into the treasure house. For the children of Israel and the children of Levi shall bring the offering." What was their initial act of obedience when revival occurred? They took care of the financial responsibilities given to them by God. Beyond that they gave freely of the first-fruits of everything they possessed.

27

2. An attached heart

When the heart is right, the treasure is poured toward God. In terms of spiritual life you must always deal with your heart attitude, because it is out of the heart that man operates. "For as he thinketh in his heart, so is he" (Prov. 23:7a). So, we preach to the heart. When the heart is right, the treasure is sent toward God. Our heart has an inseparable attachment to wherever our treasure is. Conversely, wherever our heart is, that is where we put our treasure.

Review

We are forced to make a choice. Christ gives us three choices: two treasuries, two visions, and two masters. We are forced to choose. We have to make an initial choice and follow that with a permanent choice, perhaps in a covenantal manner as did the people in Nehemiah's time. But we have to reaffirm that covenant every moment of every day. We must choose where our treasure will be, what our vision will be, and who our master will be.

I. TWO TREASURIES (vv. 19-21; see pp. 10-19)

A. The Principle (vv. 19a, 20a; see pp. 10-19)

1. Earthly treasures (v. 19a; see pp. 11-19)

"Lay not up for yourselves treasures upon earth."

The Greek word for "treasures" is *thēsaurizō*, which means "to treasure up treasures." Implicated in the meaning is a horizontal concept (i.e., something that is lying flat and stacked). A vertical concept would indicate that something is purposeful or useful. In other words, luxuries are that which we hoard or stack. It is not wrong to accumulate money and possessions to invest in divine causes and in God's purposes. God's purposes are to care for our own families, our church family, those who are not of the family of God but have need, and His causes around the world. These are needful uses of what God gives us. But to selfishly stockpile treasures for ourselves with greed and covetousness is not what our Lord wants. We should not be consumed with material wealth or labor for the food that perishes (John 6:27).

Lesson

2. Heavenly treasures (v. 20a)

"But lay up for yourselves treasures in heaven."

G. Campbell Morgan says, "You are to remember, with the passion burning within you, that you are not the child of today, you are not of the earth, you are more than dust; you are the child of tomorrow, you are of the eternities, you are the offspring of Deity. The measurements of your lives cannot be circumscribed by the point where blue sky kisses green earth. All the fact of your life cannot be encompassed in the one small sphere upon which you live. You belong to the infinite. If you make your fortune on the earth,—poor, sorry, silly soul,—you have made a fortune and stored it, in a place where you cannot hold it. Make your fortune, but store it where it will greet you in the dawning of the new morning." We cannot lay up our treasure on earth; it is not characteristic of those in His kingdom. It *was* characteristic of the Pharisees. In a sense He was saying to them, "This is just another indication that you are not in My kingdom, no matter what you claim. People in My kingdom don't lay up treasure on earth."

a) Storing the riches

The terms "treasures upon earth" and "treasures in heaven" were very familiar to the Jews. They had many sayings regarding almsgiving and piling treasure in heaven. So Jesus was speaking in a vernacular they understood. They believed that deeds of mercy and deeds of kindness to people in distress were tantamount to storing up riches in heaven.

(1) The commitment of King Monobaz

For example, the rabbis told a rather famous story about a certain king named Monobaz. When he became king he inherited incredible riches from his forefathers, the previous kings. But during the time of his reign he gave all of his fortune to the poor, the needy, the suffering, and the afflicted. His brothers went to him and said, "Thy fathers gathered treasures, and added to those of their fathers, but thou hast dispersed yours and theirs." He said this to them, "My fathers gathered treasures for below, I have gathered treasures for above; they stored treasures in a place over which the hand of man can rule, but I have stored treasures in a place over which the hand of man cannot rule; my fathers collected treasures which bear no interest, I have gathered treasures which bear interest; my fathers gathered treasures of money, I have gathered treasures in souls . . . ; my fathers gathered treasures in this world, I have gathered treasures for the world to come." The rabbis understood the concept to which our Lord referred—invest in His kingdom.

(2) The commitment of the early church

(a) During Pentecost

The early church had this commitment. They were not interested in piling up their own wealth. For example, in Acts 2 on the Day of Pentecost, there were thousands of pilgrims gathered in Jerusalem. We know from history that they would move in and live in the homes of the people who lived in the city. The city would swell with people. There were not enough inns to care for all of them, so they would move into the homes. Many of these people became believers on the great Day of Pentecost when Peter preached and 3,000 were redeemed. Thousands more were added to the church over the course of the next few chapters of Acts. Now that they were believers, they didn't want to return to their former homes because they were in the church, and there was excitement and joy in being born-again. So the believers who lived there had to absorb them. I am sure that many of them were poor and without any resources, so the early church had to give to meet their needs. As a result they sold what they possessed "as every man had need" (Acts 2:45b), in order to meet those needs.

(b) During the Decian persecution

During the time of the Decian persecution in Rome, the authorities broke into a certain church thinking they could loot their treasures. The Roman prefect who was in charge stepped up to one saint named Laurentius and said, "Show me your treasures at once." Laurentius pointed to a group of widows and orphans who happened to be eating a meal and said, "There are the treasures of the church. We have invested all we have in them." That is treasure in heaven. Remember that what we keep we lose and what we invest with God we gain eternally.

b) Securing the dividends

(1) Proverbs 3:9-10—"Honor the Lord with thy substance, and with the first fruits of all thine increase." Honor the Lord with everything you have and give Him the first part. You don't want it to be the Lord's cow that dies—give Him the first. As a result, verse 10 follows, "So shall thy barns be filled with plenty, and thy presses shall burst out with new wine." You will never be able to invest with God without receiving a dividend. You will have the investment returned plus more.

(2) Proverbs 11:24-25a—"There is he that scattereth, and yet increaseth" (v. 24a). That is what a farmer does—he throws away a little seed and receives a whole crop. Verse 24 continues, "And there is he that withholdeth more than is fitting, but it tendeth to poverty. The liberal soul shall be made fat" (vv. 24b-25a). The more you scatter, the more you receive.

(3) 2 Corinthians 9:6—"He who soweth sparingly shall reap also sparingly; and he who soweth bountifully shall reap also bountifully."

(4) Luke 6:38—"Give, and it shall be given unto you" (v. 38a). In other words, you give to God and He returns to you "good measure, pressed down, and shaken together, and running over, shall men give into your bosom. For with the same measure that ye measure it shall be measured to you again" (v. 38b). God only gives you the return on what you have invested. All of our spiritual life we will fight the battle of where to

put our treasure, luxury, and wealth. Put it in heaven and receive an eternal dividend.

c) Seeking the reward

(1) The general reward

What is our treasure in heaven? In a very broad sense, our treasure in heaven is "an inheritance incorruptible, and undefiled, and that fadeth not away, reserved in heaven for you" (1 Pet. 1:4). We could say that our treasure in heaven is Christ more than anything else. Our treasure in heaven is a faithfulness that will never be removed (Ps. 89:33; 138:8), a life that will never end (John 3:16), a love that will never cease (Rom. 8:39), a spring of water that never runs dry (John 4:14), a gift that is never lost (John 6:37, 39), and a chain that is never broken (Rom. 8:29-30).

(2) The specific reward

But in very specific terms, Jesus is talking about money, luxury, and wealth:

(a) 1 Timothy 6:17-19—"Charge them that are rich in this age, that they be not highminded [don't let your riches make you proud], nor trust in uncertain riches but in the living God, who giveth us richly all things to enjoy" (v. 17). Now, we have the wealth, but what are we to do with it?

Verse 18 says, "That they do good, that they be rich in good works, ready to distribute, willing to share." The call of God upon our lives regarding our luxuries and wealth is that we distribute and share as opposed to hoarding and stockpiling.

As a result, verse 19a says, "Laying up in store [Gk., *thēsaurizō* = 'treasuring up treasure'] for themselves." What does it mean to put treasure in heaven? It means to distribute and to share the riches God has given to us. In that way we put together "a good foundation against the time to come, that they [we] may lay hold on eternal life" (v. 19b). In other words, we expose ourselves to the full potential of all that eternal life can mean. The more

I send into glory, the greater the glory when I arrive. The greater the investment, the greater the reward.

(b) Luke 12:33a—"Sell what ye have, and give alms; provide yourselves bags which grow not old." In other words, don't just stick your money into bags that are going to rot and decay; put your money into bags that will never grow old, "a treasure in the heavens that faileth not."

(c) Luke 16:9—"And I say unto you, Make to yourselves friends by means of the money of unrighteousness, that, when it fails, they may receive you into everlasting habitations." Money is basically an unrighteous commodity. Now that is not disparaging or damning it; it is just stating that money has no righteous virtue. So as long as you have an unrighteous commodity to begin with— something that has no righteous virtue—use it to make yourself friends (i.e., invest your money in the souls of people) who someday will greet you with thanksgiving when you step on the shore of heaven. What a fabulous thought and promise! What are you going to do with your treasure? Whatever you keep here you lose; whatever you send ahead by investing in the lives and the souls of men you gain forever.

(d) Proverbs 19:17—"He that hath pity upon the poor lendeth unto the Lord" (v. 17a). What is the basic principle of a loan? You will be paid back. So, when you have pity on the poor and lend to the Lord, verse 17b says, "and that which he hath given will he pay him again." Don't be earthbound, don't put treasure in this world, and don't stockpile here; invest it in eternity.

B. The Reasons (vv. 19b, 20b-21)

1. The earthly problems (vv. 19b, 20b)

"Where moth and rust doth corrupt, and where thieves break through and steal . . . where neither moth nor

33

rust doth corrupt, and where thieves do not break through nor steal."

We should choose the heavenly treasury, where there is no moth or rust and where thieves don't break through and steal. In the Orient during biblical times, wealth was basically preserved in three ways. There was no paper, there were no bank books, there was nothing to match the kind of system we have. Wealth was identified in literal commodities: garments, grain, and gold or precious metal.

a)   Garments

   (1)   The possession of garments

   In biblical times, garments were a very important commodity.

   (*a*)   Gehazi—He was the servant of Elisha who wished to make some forbidden profit out of Naaman's leprosy cure. So he asked for a talent of silver and two changes of garments, because that was substantial wealth (2 Kings 5:22). Wealth was expressed in fancy, rich, extravagant garments.

   (*b*)   Achan—In Joshua 7:21 he says, "When I saw among the spoils a beautiful Babylonish garment . . . then I coveted them, and took them."

   (*c*)   Joseph—When he bestowed upon Benjamin his affection, he gave him five changes of garments (Gen. 45:22).

   (*d*)   Samson—To the Philistines he said, "If you can answer the riddle, I promise you thirty garments and thirty changes of garments" (Judg. 14:12).

   Garments were always an expression of wealth because they were a commodity of great value. Very often gold was woven into the garment. In addition, the dyeing processes could be unique, so some were very fancy. Also, the material was hard to make.

   (2)   The problem with garments

   There is one problem with garments—moths eat them. We have mothballs to prevent that. But have you ever noticed that moths don't eat what you wear, only what you store? We tend to hoard, and a lot of our treasure is invested in our garments, waiting for the moths to corrupt (lit., "consume") them.

b) Grain

Another way they stored their wealth was in grain. The rich fool said, "I will pull down my barns, and build greater; and there will I bestow all my crops and my goods" (Luke 12:18b). His wealth was in grain. The word "rust" in Matthew 6:19-20 actually means "eating." Nowhere in the Bible is it used to mean rust. The Greek word *brōsis* basically means "eating." The problem with grain is that mice, rats, worms, and vermin like to eat it. Fifteen percent of all of the stored grain of India is eaten by rats and mice.

c) Gold

The third commodity they put their treasure into was gold or precious metal. The problem with that is this: How do you hide it? You might keep it in your house, but a thief could break in and steal it. The most common thing that was done was to find a secret place in their field, and in the dark of night dig a hole and bury it. Matthew 13:44 gives the parable of the man who found the treasure stored in a field. But thieves would lurk around at night and watch where men would bury their treasure and then go and dig it up. In addition, when a thief broke into a house, he would literally dig through the wall. The phrase "thieves break through" literally means "to dig through." The thieves were mud diggers literally digging through the wall of a house or the dirt in the ground.

So, your garments could be eaten by moths, your grain could be eaten by animals or insects, and your gold could be taken by mud diggers. The point is this: If you hoard it, you can lose it because it is unsafe and insecure.

Today we have mothballs, rat poison, and burglar alarms, and still none of our wealth is very safe. You are better off sending it into the kingdom and reaping the eternal rewards. People say, "Well, I have mine in a bank." Those of you who went through the Depression know how secure banks are. There is no place of security in this life. Even if you kept it all until you died, you would still leave it behind.

2. The heavenly perspective (v. 21)

"For where your treasure is, there will your heart be also."

Where is your heart? There are many millionaires who will be paupers in eternity, and there are paupers in this life who will be millionaires forever. Where is your treasure? Is it always the Lord's cow that dies, or do you invest in His kingdom?

II. TWO VISIONS (vv. 22-23)

A. The Explanation (vv. 22-23a)

"The lamp of the body is the eye; if, therefore, thine eye be healthy, thy whole body shall be full of light. But if thine eye be evil, thy whole body shall be full of darkness."

Jesus wants us to have our heart fixed single-mindedly and totally on the kingdom of God so that our treasure, heart, love, passion, burden, and investment is with the kingdom. He illustrates the single-minded heart with the eye.

1. The principle (v. 22a)

"The lamp of the body is the eye."

When sighted people see with their eyes, their body is filled with the light that comes in from the world that they perceive through their vision. But if their eye is dark, there is no light and they perceive nothing. The same thing is true of the heart. If your heart is toward God, your entire spiritual being is enlightened, but if your heart is toward the material things and the treasure of the world, the blinds come down on your spiritual perception and you do not see spiritually as you should. Jesus said the eye is like a window—if the window is clean and clear, light floods the body; but if the window is blacked out, no light enters.

2. The reasons (vv. 22b-23a)

a) The single eye (v. 22b)

"If, therefore, thine eye be healthy, thy whole body shall be full of light."

(1) The meaning

The word "healthy" is literally from the root of the Greek word *haplous*, which means "generous." It is used that way many times.

(*a*) James 1:5*b*—"God, who giveth to all men liberally."

(*b*) Romans 12:8—Paul urges us to give "with liberality."

(*c*) 2 Corinthians 9:13—The Macedonians gave liberally, or generously.

So He is saying that if your heart is generous, your whole spiritual life will be flooded with spiritual understanding.

(2) The misappropriation

There are people who come to church and never seem to change. They never grow, never seem to love the Word, never seem to be a witness to others, and never seem to be productive in their lives. When I see someone who never seems to understand spiritual realities, I wonder if it isn't because he is so focused on the earth and oriented toward earthly treasures that the blinds are down and he has no spiritual perception.

To put it another way, until you take care of the view of money in your life, you will never be able to deal with spiritual realities. Luke 16:11 says that if you don't know how to take care of money, why should God commit to you the true riches? Our Lord is saying that this issue is so big that it may be blinding our spiritual perception.

b) The evil eye (v. 23*a*)

"But if thine eye be evil, thy whole body shall be full of darkness."

Here we are introduced to the "evil eye." The "evil eye" is a Jewish colloquialism. The Greek word *ponēros* is actually used regularly in the Septuagint and in the New Testament to mean "grudgingly."

(1) Proverbs 23:6a—"Eat thou not the bread of him who hath an evil eye." In other words, don't eat a bite of somebody's food if he grudges you every bite.

(2) Proverbs 28:22—"He that hasteneth to be rich hath an evil eye, and considereth not that poverty shall come upon him." If you hurry to be rich you will be ungenerous, grudging, and selfish.

There are two treasuries—you either have one in heaven or one in the earth. Wherever you put your treasure is where your heart will be. If your heart is in heaven you will have a generous spirit. That generous spirit is like a seeing eye that floods your spiritual life with perception. If your treasure is on earth you are going to see nothing because the blinds come down in the darkness of your greed and covetousness.

B. The Exclamation (v. 23b)

"If, therefore, the light that is in thee be darkness, how great is that darkness!"

This is just an exclamation: How total is the darkness of one who should see spiritually but pulls down the blinds because of his own covetousness!

The call is to exclusive heavenly-mindedness, devotion to God, and an undivided laying up of treasure in heaven. Let me simplify it to one statement: How you handle your money is the key to your spiritual perception. So, you can make a choice between two treasuries, two visions, and finally:

III. TWO MASTERS (v. 24)

"No man can serve two masters; for either he will hate the one, and love the other; or else he will hold to the one, and despise the other. Ye cannot serve God and money."

A. The Principle

People always say, "I don't believe that you can't serve two masters. I work two jobs. I can serve two masters." The reason people say that is they don't understand the word "serve." It does not refer to an employee in an eight-to-five job. It is the Greek word *douleuō*, from which we get *doulos*, which is the word for "bondslave." You can't be a slave to two masters.

B.   The Reasons

1.   Required responsibilities

Slavery, by definition, means "single ownership and full-time service." A slave was not a person; a slave was a thing and had no rights. A master could beat a slave, sell a slave, or kill a slave. A slave was a living tool, no different than a plow or a cow. To be a bondslave—to be the property of a master—was to be constantly, totally, entirely, 100 percent devoted to obedience to that one master. It would be utterly impossible to express that obedience to two different masters.

a)   Exclusive devotion

According to Romans 6:16-18, now that we have come to Christ, we must yield ourselves as servants to Him because we are His slaves and no longer the slaves of sin. God can only be served with entire and exclusive devotion, with single-mindedness. If you try to split that devotion with money, you will hate one or the other.

b)   Eliminating division

Some of you may be hoarding your money. You have been selfish and not investing it in God's causes or giving it to those in need. Instead, you have just been piling it on for yourself. Now, as you are exposed to God's Word, you are beginning to resent God's claim on your life. You are fighting that because you can't serve those two things. On the other hand, if everything you own you want to give to God, if every treasure you own in this world you want to pour out to Him, then you despise the system that takes so much away from you. It will bother you that gas prices keep going up because that is infringing on what you want to invest eternally. You can't serve both—you have to choose your master.

2.   Opposite orders

The orders of these two masters are diametrically opposed. The one commands you to walk by faith, the other to walk by sight; the one to be humble, the other to be proud; the one to set your affections on things above, the other to set them on the things of the earth; the one to look at the things unseen and eternal, the other to look at the things seen and temporal; the one to have your conversation in heaven, the other to cleave to the dust; the one to be careful for nothing, the other to be all anxiety. They are diametrically opposed—you can't serve them both.

a) Bishop Ryle—He said, "Singleness of purpose is the greatest secret of spiritual prosperity." It is that absolute focus that makes you spiritually rich.

b) Caleb—He put it this way, "I wholly followed the Lord my God" (Josh. 14:8b).

c) David—He puts it this way in Psalm 16:8a, "I have set the Lord always before me."

Where is the safest place to put your treasure? Where you will have the clearest spiritual sight and where you will be able to serve the right Master. The possession of wealth is not a sin, but it is a great responsibility. Sometimes I wish I were poor so I wouldn't have that responsibility. But poor people have their problems, too. John Calvin said, "Where riches hold the dominion of the heart, God has lost His authority." That is the issue. If I have my choice, I will take the money I have and give it to friends who someday will meet me when I enter the eternal habitation. M. E. Byrne said, "Riches I heed not, nor man's empty praise; Thou mine inheritance, now and always."

Focusing on the Facts

1. What is the critical issue of an individual's spiritual life? What will it determine (see p. 25)?
2. Explain how the Pharisees revealed the true location of their hearts (see p. 25).
3. What is the key verse of the Sermon on the Mount? What is the contrast that it points out in regard to the hearts of the Pharisees (see p. 25)?
4. What is one of the results of a right heart (see p. 26)?
5. How was the revival initiated in Nehemiah 8:1 (see p. 26)?
6. What four things came as a result of reading the law? What kind of decision is encompassed in these four things (see pp. 26-27)?
7. What was the covenant that the people of Israel made with God (see p. 27)?
8. What happens to our treasure when we have a right heart attitude (see p. 28)?
9. Why were the terms "treasures upon earth" and "treasures in heaven" very familiar to the Jews? Support your answer with some examples (see pp. 29-30).

10. How did the early church manifest the location of its heart (see pp. 30-31)?
11. What is our treasure in heaven, in a general sense (see p. 32)?
12. What is our treasure in heaven specifically? Support your answer (see pp. 32-33).
13. How can we use the unrighteous money we have as a benefit to others and ourselves (see p. 33)?
14. What were the three ways in which wealth was preserved in the Orient (see p. 34)?
15. Explain the problems that were encountered by the people in preserving their wealth in these three ways (see pp. 34-35).
16. What is the main problem with hoarding wealth (see p. 35)?
17. Explain how the eye can be the lamp of the body. How does it relate to the heart (see p. 36)?
18. Explain the meaning of the single eye (see p. 37).
19. What is the result of not having the right view of money (see p. 37)?
20. Explain the meaning of the evil eye. Support your answer (see pp. 37-38).
21. Why can't an individual be a slave to two masters (see p. 39)?
22. Explain how the orders of the two masters are diametrically opposed (see pp. 39-40).
23. Where is the safest place to put your treasure (see p. 40)?

Pondering the Principles

1. What is your response when you read the Word of God? Are you convicted of your sin and then willing to confess that sin? Do you have a desire to obey God? Do you offer praise to God as a result of reading His Word? Finally, do you promise to walk in a new direction after your encounter with God? A reading of His Word should produce these four things in your life. See if these things really do occur by having a Bible study right now. Look up the following verses: Proverbs 3:9-10; 11:24-25; Luke 6:38; 12:33; 16:9; 2 Corinthians 9:6; 1 Timothy 6:17-19. As you study, confess any sin that the Holy Spirit convicts you of. See if you do not have a greater desire to obey God. Offer up praise to Him for His Word. Finally, the most important part of Bible study is application. What changes do you need to make in your life regarding the priority of riches? As the nation of Israel became obedient when they heard the reading of the law (Nehemiah 8:5-6, 8), you should be obedient to God.

2. If you stand in a room that is completely dark, what can you see?

What kind of feeling do you experience when you stand in a completely dark room? Compare this to how you felt before you became a Christian. What did you understand about spiritual things? How did your understanding change when you came to Christ? The same thing is true now with regard to how you see spiritually. What kind of spiritual eye do you have? Do you have a healthy, generous eye, or do you have an evil, grudging eye? Be honest as you examine yourself. If you are more grudging than generous, you are missing out on many exciting spiritual blessings. Ask God to show you how you might become a more generous individual.

3. To better understand the fact that you have changed your master, memorize Romans 6:17-18: "But God be thanked, that whereas ye were the servants of sin, ye have obeyed from the heart that form of doctrine which was delivered you. Being, then, made free from sin, ye became the servants of righteousness."

3
Mastery of Materialism

Outline

Introduction
A. The Passages
  1. Matthew 6:25-34
  2. Matthew 6:19-24
B. The Perspective

Lesson
I. The Test of Spirituality
  A. The Trauma of Technology
    1. The product—unlimited resources
    2. The problem—ultimate self-destruction
  B. The Trap of Technology
    1. The philosophy of the world
      a) Seeking the assets
      b) Stealing the assets
    2. The philosophy of Christianity
II. The Treasure of Contentment
  A. The Trust of Contentment
    1. Ownership
      a) The passages
        (1) Psalm 24:1*a*
        (2) 1 Chronicles 29:11*b*
      b) The pattern
        (1) A smashed van
        (2) A burned house
      c) The principle
    2. Control
      a) 1 Chronicles 29:11*b*-12
      b) Daniel 2:20-21*a*
      c) Daniel 6
    3. Provision

B. The Test of Contentment
   1. Meeting the need
   2. Releasing the resources
   3. Pouring the treasure
III. The Trials of Materialism
   A. Posh Christianity
   B. Posh Pastors
   C. Posh Guests

Introduction

A. The Passages

    1. Matthew 6:25-34

Here is the setting for our lesson: "Therefore, I say unto you, Be not anxious for your life, what ye shall eat, or what ye shall drink; nor yet for your body, what ye shall put on. Is not the life more than food and the body than raiment? Behold the fowls of the air; for they sow not, neither do they reap, nor gather into barns, yet your heavenly Father feedeth them. Are ye not much better than they? Which of you by being anxious can add one cubit unto his stature? And why are ye anxious for raiment? Consider the lilies of the field, how they grow; they toil not, neither do they spin, and yet I say unto you that even Solomon, in all his glory, was not arrayed like one of these. Wherefore, if God so clothe the grass of the field, which today is, and tomorrow is cast into the oven, shall he not much more clothe you, O ye of little faith? Therefore, be not anxious saying, What shall we eat? or, What shall we drink? or, With what shall we be clothed? For after all these things do the Gentiles seek. For your heavenly Father knoweth that ye have need of all these things. But seek ye first the kingdom of God, and his righteousness, and all these things shall be added unto you. Be, therefore, not anxious about tomorrow; for tomorrow will be anxious for the things of itself. Sufficient unto the day is its own evil."

    2. Matthew 6:19-24

"Lay not up for yourselves treasures upon earth, where moth and rust doth corrupt, and where thieves break through and steal, but lay up for yourselves treasures in heaven, where neither moth nor rust doth corrupt, and where thieves do not break through nor steal; for where your treasure is, there will your heart be also. The lamp of the body is the eye; if, therefore, thine eye be healthy, thy whole body shall be full of light. But if thine eye be evil, thy whole body shall be full of darkness. If, therefore, the light that is in thee be darkness, how great is that darkness! No man can serve two masters; for either he will hate the one, and love the other; or else he will hold to the one and despise the other. Ye cannot serve God and money."

B. The Perspective

Both of these passages deal with physical commodities and material possessions. Verses 19-24 deal with luxury, and verses 25-34 deal with necessity—what we eat, drink, and wear. The first portion is directed more to the rich—those who tend to take their luxury and stockpile it for their own ends. The second is directed more to the poor who, due to their poverty and lack of substance, question or doubt God and live in anxiety about what they will eat, drink, and wear.

Now, being rich has its share of problems, just as being poor has its share. The temptation to the rich is to trust in riches, whereas the temptation to the poor is to doubt God's provision. But in both cases the Lord is saying, "I have a perspective for you. Whether you are rich or poor, your focus is to be on Me." For example, in verse 21 He says, "Put your treasure in heaven because that is where I want your heart." In verse 33a He says, "But seek ye first the kingdom." In other words, "Put your heart in heaven and don't worry; I will give you what you need. I want you to have a focus." The focus of the rich in the world is to lay up treasures on earth (v. 19). The focus of the poor in the world is to seek after what they will eat, drink, and wear for clothing. If you are rich, pursue a heavenly investment; if you are poor, pursue the kingdom of God. When it comes to money and possessions, our focus is to be on God and not on possessions. We are not to grasp and claw after things; we are to seek God and allow Him to fulfill His promises to us.

Now, I want to give you an introduction to the second section (vv. 25-34), which deals with necessities.

Lesson

I. THE TEST OF SPIRITUALITY

Managing money and possessions is a severe problem for all of us. We all have different amounts of money by God's design. But we all have the same problem: What do we do with it? How should we invest it? How should we spend it? We have to constantly face the fact that money provides for us a test of true spirituality. I can tell you more about the spirituality of a man or woman simply by the way he handles his physical properties. It is a great revealer of the heart. It is a major problem in life, and when somebody can deal with it, the strength of his spiritual life is manifested.

For example, the Lord told thirty-eight parables in the gospels. Out of those thirty-eight, sixteen concern how we handle our money. Christ said more about money and possessions than about heaven and hell combined. In the gospels, 1 out of every 10 verses deals with money or possessions—288 verses in the four gospels. In the Bible there are more than 500 references to prayer and less than 500 references to faith, but there are more than 2,000 references to money and possessions. It is a major issue.

A. The Trauma of Technology

1. The product—unlimited resources

   It is not any easier for us now than it was in Bible times— if anything, it's tougher. We live in a day when technology has provided for us an incredible amount of unlimited resources. For example, there has never been a society in the history of the world that has had as many commodities and products as we have. And in America, we probably have more than any other part of the world. We are living in affluence that is unheard of in the world's history. Modern technology has increased our comprehension of devices and designs to the point where we can now create almost anything short of life itself.

2. The problem—ultimate self-destruction

   But our incredible affluence and development of commodities has revealed a major problem: man cannot handle what he produces. We cannot handle our money or our commodities. In the very simplest sense, we are in the process of ultimate self-destruction. Now, all of us are very much aware of where our country and the world are going with all of the economic and financial problems we have. But the problem is not economic or financial. That is why nobody can come up with the right solution.

The problem is this: If man creates an environment with unlimited commodities, man will destroy himself. There is a basic truth about man that must be recognized: He is ultimately and totally selfish. Selfishness related to productivity translates into one word—greed. When the sinful heart of man is egged on by selfishness and attaches itself to products, it becomes greed, and self-destruction is the ultimate end. For example, in Revelation 18 the entire world economic system ends in total collapse. Man is on a track to total self-destruction. When man continues to proliferate the potential to make money and proliferate products, he is given that which feeds the worst thing about him—his selfishness and greed.

B. The Trap of Technology

We are maniacal in our desire for things. We are egged on by the media, and man is trapped in the unbelievable hyprocrisy of the system. He has been told all of his life that he can be happy only when he obtains all the commodities he possibly can. Now society tells him he cannot have them. So, he is being forced to be unhappy. We are in this mess because this society produced its potential with the help of the evil of man's heart. Through television, radio, and billboards this society has been telling us that we will be happy when we have things. Now they tell us that we can't have our things.

1. The philosophy of the world

The key philosophy of life in the world is this: Only as you accumulate enough assets to satisfy your particular style of life can you really be happy. We have a society of people who have determined what assets they want. We even have subcultures who desire strange things.

a) Seeking the assets

I saw on a man's shirt a sign I could not believe: "Next to sex, I like Harley-Davidsons best." That is the way he read life. If he could just get enough money to get the right girl and the right machine, he was happy—he thought. If we can just get a fancier car, a new wardrobe, take a trip, or get a bigger house we can be happy. This is exactly what the media pumps at us all the time. We see the big ads that say they are going to put a "Caspar Milquetoast" into this

47

hot car and he will turn into a macho man whom all the girls will scream at as he goes down the street. If you look kind of tacky around the house in your bathrobe, just buy the new fashions.

b) Stealing for assets

People say, "There is so much thievery today. Why, man is getting worse." That is not the issue. When he is continually told that he has to have commodities to be happy, ultimately he is going to steal for them.

I am not interested in the world's solution because it is full of hypocrisy. When society tells me to tighten my belt and to change my standard of living, I say, "That is not the issue. It is only the periphery. You have told us that we will never be happy until we can absorb the assets to make our style of life what we seek. Now that we have decided to live that way, you tell us not to. That is hypocritical!" Man has been lied to all along.

2. The philosophy of Christianity

Sad to say, Christians have bought this philosophy. We even think that happiness comes in commodities. Christianity has become big business. Richard Quebedeaux says that Christians are guilty of upward social mobility. We are trying so hard to climb the ladder to hobnob with the rich and famous. But that is not what our Lord said. Our heart is to be in heaven because our treasure is there. We will not find happiness in our lives in commodities. Now, I am not against those commodities; I just don't seek for them. If God chooses to give us things, it is due to His good and gracious hand; but if we make those things the love of our lives, we have missed His blessing because we have been lied to about where real contentment is found.

Philippians 4:11-12 paraphrased says, "Not that I was ever in need, for I have learned how to get along happily whether I have much or little. I know how to live on almost nothing or with everything. I have learned the secret of contentment in every situation, whether it be a full stomach or hunger, plenty or want" (TLB*). Paul says, "I have contentment that is absolutely and totally unrelated to possessions." The believer seeks the king-

*The Living Bible.

48

dom, and God takes care of the possessions; he puts his treasure in heaven, and the Lord takes care of his needs.

II. THE TREASURE OF CONTENTMENT

Jesus directed much of His speaking to the covetous Pharisees and scribes. They were in it for the money. They had turned the Temple into a prospering business. They were rich, and they had the jaded perspective of the world that you will be happy and content only when you have accumulated enough wealth to satisfy your desired life-style.

A. The Trust of Contentment

The Bible says that contentment is apart from goods and commodities. Your contentment is found in God. There are three words that relate to the issue of contentment with God:

1. Ownership

God is the sole owner of everything. He owns your clothes, your shoes, your watch, your house, your car, your kids, your garden—everything. He owns it all.

a) The passages

(1) Psalm 24:1*a*—"The earth belongs to God! Everything in all the world is his!" (TLB).

(2) 1 Chronicles 29:11*b*—"Everything in the heavens and earth is yours, O Lord, and this is your kingdom" (TLB). If I am going to be content in life as a Christian, then the first thing I have to realize is that everything belongs to God. As a result, I can never gain anything because it is already His. In order to learn to be content you must recognize that God is the sole owner of everything.

b) The pattern

If you believe for one minute that you own one single possession, then that possession will govern your spiritual attitudes. Let me give you two illustrations:

(1) A smashed van

We have a van that we enjoy as a family because we have four kids. Now I think it is important to take care of that van because it costs a lot to buy another one. If I say, "This is *my* van. I'm going to take care of *my* van," and *my* van is traveling along the road when somebody comes through

49

an intersection and smashes *my* van, then I am going to be very upset with the person that ran into *my* van. Then I am going to find out the inevitable—he has no insurance, and my sanctification will flee further from my grasp. Then I am going to take it to the body shop, and they won't match the paint properly, and I will get it back with a big streak on the side, so then I will be upset with them. Then I will be traveling down the street at an angle because the frame was bent, and that will wear out my tires and cost me money. But it is not my van, so if somebody runs into it I say, "Lord, You should be careful how You take care of Your van. Sorry this happened to Your van. I hope You have the resources to get it fixed." I have to deal with things in my life either from my perspective or His. As long as it is His, I don't worry.

(2) A burned house

John Wesley was away from home one day when a terrible tragedy was reported to him: his house had just burned down. He said, "The Lord's house burned down. One less responsibility for me."

c) The principle

That is the right approach, but it is not what we have been taught. The accumulation of property is the legacy of the world to us, and we need to change that perspective. We do not own anything. I don't own my house, my car, or my children. Therefore, if I lose something, I don't really lose it, because I never owned it. If someone needs something, he is just as welcome to it as I am, because I don't own it—the Lord does. If the Lord knows others need it—it's theirs. I have to begin with the understanding that God owns everything. But that is a problem for Americans, because the concept of capitalism and the right to ownership of private property is an American legacy. We are so willing to stand up and fight for it that we forget that it is not a Christian principle.

The Elements of Stewardship

In 1914 a man named Harvey Calkins wrote a book entitled *The Elements of Stewardship*. He said that we have received a heritage of ownership from our society and not from the Bible. He said, "There has been but one nation whose concept of property ownership was based on ownership by a personal God, and that nation was Israel. All the other nations we have knowledge of—the Egyptians, the Greeks, and the Romans—their underlying philosophy of the ownership of property and their laws relating to property were based on the concept of the individual owning what he possessed.

"Where did we receive our standards of property ownership? It is rooted in the law of the Roman empire. The Roman philosophy of life, crystallized in Roman law and through that law standardized in Christian civilization, was not built on 'the law of the Lord—ownership by God'; it was based on the laws of man—ownership by man.

"The average man, unless he has met the issues squarely and jarred himself loose from inherited traditions, remains caught in a false concept of property ownership. His Christian instinct is entangled with the honest belief that he is the owner of what he has merely been given to possess. His whole history and entire culture compel him to believe that he is the owner of his property." That is not true because, in a real sense, you don't own anything and neither do I. If I don't own anything, then I don't mind if I lose it.

2. Control

The first thing you have to understand is that God owns everything; the second thing is that He controls everything. He is the Owner and the Controller. For example, the Old Testament gives special attention to the fact that God controls all circumstances for His own ends:

a) 1 Chronicles 29:11b-12—"We adore you as being in control of everything. Riches and honor come from you alone, and you are the Ruler of all mankind; your hand controls power and might, and it is at your discretion that men are made great and given strength" (TLB). In other words, "God, You control everything. You control riches, You control honor, You control power and might and greatness and strength. You call all the shots."

51

b) Daniel 2:20-21*a*—"Blessed be the name of God forever and ever, for he alone has all wisdom and all power. World events are under his control" (TLB).

c) Daniel 6—When Daniel was thrown into the lions' den, this kind of theology held him in good stead, even though he was in utterly terrible circumstances. I can't imagine anything worse than being dropped into a pit with a bunch of hungry lions. There were enough of those lions to devour a whole family of relatives before they hit the bottom of the pit. Daniel had a wonderful time—he was at ease, relaxed; he probably lay down on a nice big furry lion and went to sleep. Meanwhile, the king, who was in perfect circumstances, living in the Babylonian palace as the greatest monarch in the world, couldn't eat, sleep, drink, or be entertained. Why? Daniel knew that in everything God was in total control. The other man was a wreck because he had no sense of a divine Controller, and the circumstances were beyond his control.

If you know God owns and controls everything, then you will not put your hope in luxury, and you will not fear for your needs. God knows what you need—He will provide for all your needs "according to his riches in glory by Christ Jesus" (Phil. 4:19*b*). He will take care of everything that is necessary for your life. God will dispense to you what He knows you must have in order to invest in His kingdom. That is not your worry.

3. Provision

Ownership, control, and provision. God owns everything, and He controls everything to provide for His own.

The Old Testament gives God many names, but one of the most lovely of the names of God is *Jehovah-jireh* (Gen. 22:14). It means "the Lord who provides." It is so much a characteristic of God that it is His name. We would never argue that God is love and glorious and great and mighty and holy and just and good, but some would argue whether God provides. They question and doubt and are afraid that God isn't going to meet their needs. This is exactly what the Lord speaks to in Matthew 6:25-34 when He says, "Don't worry about what to eat, drink, or wear." The Lord is still *Jehovah-jireh*. That is His name and it is synonymous with one of His attributes.

God is a God who provides, and that is why David said, "I have never seen God's people begging bread" (Ps. 37:25b). Paraphrased, Luke 12:30 says, "All mankind scratches for its daily bread" (TLB). The world digs and scratches and claws and hoards to make sure it has enough, but, in opposition, your Father knows your needs and He will always give you what you need and He will always give you what you need every day. What a promise!

I don't have to own everything, and I don't have to control everything in order to meet my needs. I can receive what God gives me to invest in His eternal kingdom and put away all anxiety about my needs. I can worship God with my life and have the absolute promise that He will provide everything beyond what I need. First Timothy 6:8 says, "And if we have food and covering, with these we shall be content" (NASB*). Are you content, or do you grasp for more and deny God in the process?

A Little Piece of Bread

In World War II the death of many adults left many orphans. At the close of the war, the allies provided some camps for the orphans in order to feed them and to try to find a place to locate them. They began to develop and grow. They received the finest care and the finest food. But in one of these camps the officials became very perplexed because the children couldn't sleep. They would eat three good meals, but at night they would lie awake. They brought in some psychologists to do a study of these orphans to find our why they couldn't sleep.

The psychologists came up with a solution. Every night when the little children were put to bed, someone would come down the row of beds and place in each little hand a piece of bread. So, the last thing they would experience at night would be to close that little hand around the bread. In a matter of days they were all sleeping through the night. Why? Even though they were fed to the full during the day, experience had taught them that there was no hope for tomorrow. They couldn't sleep because of anxiety over what might happen the next day. They could not enjoy what they had because they were afraid of the future. When they had

*New American Standard Bible.

that bread tucked in their hands, they knew that at least they would have breakfast the next day.

Do you know what God has done for us? I believe He has given us a piece of bread for our hand. That little piece of bread is this: "But my God shall supply all your need according to his riches in glory by Christ Jesus" (Phil. 4:19). If I have that little piece of bread in my hand, I can sleep.

I don't need to stockpile for the future. God is the owner of everything in the world, and He controls all the assets to provide for me because I am His child. That is why the Lord says, "Don't you know that your heavenly Father feeds the birds, and are you not much better than they?" (Matt. 6:26). If He feeds birds, He will certainly feed His own children. He is the Owner, the Controller, and the Provider. Life for the Christian consists not in the abundance of things we possess (Luke 12:15b) but in being content with such things as we have (Heb. 13:5b).

B. The Test of Contentment

If the Lord chooses to give me more, that is fine. I have to remember that it is His and it should be used for His glory and for His kingdom.

1. Meeting the need

Sometimes when I recognize a need, somebody says to me, "What about the future? You might run out of food. You don't know what might happen. Your children might get sick." But if someone has a need and I have the resource to meet that need, that is no decision for me. I am going to take the resource that God owns and use it in His way to provide for the one in need. In the future God will have to provide for me in another way.

2. Releasing the resources

Some people can't make that decision. We tend to stock-pile inordinate amounts. Now it is not wrong to plan for the future—I think God expects us to. The book of Proverbs affirms this. But, when you cling to your possessions, when your hope and faith are in them, and when you live in fear of not having them, then you can't release them because you feel they are yours. When I see a need and someone makes an appeal, there is just something in me that wants to give in that direction. I don't always think about the future. Short of being foolish, I think that is the way we have to learn to live.

3. Pouring the treasure

Amassing money and possessions provides no contentment. To be contented is to pour your treasure into a
heavenly vault where it will pay eternal dividends. To be
content is to not worry about what you eat, or drink, or
what you shall wear, but to hold in your hand that little
piece of bread that says, "My God shall supply all your
needs" (Phil. 4:19). Then whatever resources I do have, I
will make available to whoever needs them.

So, a right relationship with God is at the bottom of true
contentment—trusting Him as Owner, Controller, and Provider.
The Bible's answer to inflation, to greed, to stealing, to selfishness, and to pride is to believe that God will meet your every
need. After all, He is your Father. I daresay that the reason those
little orphans were afraid was that they were orphans. They
didn't have a father to provide—we do.

III. THE TRIALS OF MATERIALISM

It is not wrong to have possessions. It is not wrong to have
money. But it is wrong to covet, cling, and build your life around
them. I believe that this is a major issue facing the church today.
Christianity, instead of offering an alternative, instead of being
distinct, and instead of being apart from the world, has become
materialist and self-indulgent in many ways. It is a fearful thing.
I am not sure that Christians are willing to be the offscouring of
the world anymore (1 Cor. 4:13).

A. Posh Christianity

John White has written a very helpful book called *The Golden
Cow*. In it he says that we have bowed down to the golden
cow of materialism and we need Christ to make a whip and
cleanse the Temple all over again. He also says:

"Not a calf, if you please, but a cow. I call her a *golden* cow
because her udders are engorged with liquid gold, especially
in the West where she grazes in meadows lush with green-
backs. Her priests placate her by slaughtering godly principles upon whose blood she looks with tranquil satisfaction.
Anxious rows of worshipers bow down before their buckets.
Although the gold squirts endlessly the worshipers are
trembling lest the supply of sacrificial victims should one day
fail to appease her. . . .

"Fundamentalism is my mother. I was nurtured in her warm
bosom. She cared for me with love and taught me all she

knew. I owe her (humanly speaking) my life, my spiritual food and many of my early joys. She introduced me to the Savior and taught me to feed on the bread of life. Our relationship wasn't all honey and roses, but she was the only mother I had. I clung to her then and find it hard not to lean on her now. If she let me down at times I'm old enough to realize that no mother is perfect. But to find out that she was a whore, that she let herself be used by mammon, was another matter. And as the wider evangelical movement gradually took her place in my life it was painful to make the same discovery twice" (John White, *The Golden Cow* [Downers Grove, Ill.: InterVarsity, 1979], pp. 67-68).

That is very potent and true. I believe that churches today face a tremendous amount of collective materialism on the part of their members. We are all like the man in Luke 12:16-18 whom the Bible says kept building bigger and bigger barns. This is not for Christians. Where can we get our distinctness if we fall prey to the thinking that so dominates the world?

B. Posh Pastors

I am not saying we are to be poor. For example, take the preacher. Some people think the preacher ought to be very poor—that it will make him into a man of prayer. Other people think the preacher ought to be very rich, because he will attract rich people who will feed the budget.

John White talks about this: "What would be wrong with giving him fifty percent more than whatever sum seems reasonable? Are you afraid it might make *him* too money conscious? If so, what business did you have in appointing him? If you are in a position to pick a pastor, you should also know that God expects you to discern whether he has a weakness about money. And if he has a weakness about money, you should never have given him the responsibility of a pastorate (1 Tim. 3:3)!"

"Some churches like to give high salaries because the pastor's standard of living will affect the kind of people who will attend. (Posh pastor; fancy congregation.) God is concerned with motives not with amounts. Do you resent the thought of your pastor having too much money? Then double his salary! Why! To show him you love him. But aren't there better ways of showing love? Of course there are, but why not show him love in these ways too? Do you ask me what happens if the salary is too much for him? I answer, that's the pastor's problem. He could give more money away, for instance. Pray that he may have wisdom in handling what he doesn't need" (John White, *The Golden Cow* [Downers Grove, Ill.: InterVarsity, 1979], pp. 89-90).

Grace Community Church pays me too much money. Several years ago I asked one of the elders, "Why do you pay me so much money?" He said, "Because we want to see what you do with what you don't need." That's fair. I have that responsibility. It is not a question of how much you have; it's a question of where your heart is.

C. Posh Guests

It is amazing, but in Christianity today there are people who want to come and speak at our church for a minimum fee of $5,000. There are people who want to come and sing, and they charge $8,000 and up. Now not all of them are like that. But there are even people who will give a testimony for Christ for $1,500. I talked to a publisher recently who told me that in order to get an author to write a Christian book for them they had to pay him a $200,000 advance before he would sign on the dotted line. Books are a wonderful ministry, but if you write a book to make money, that is a wrong motive. If you write a book to honor God and to advance His kingdom, and He chooses to give you money, that is the right motive and the result is a blessing. Then use that money as His possession under His control to provide for His body.

You don't need all your money and possessions to meet your needs, because God will do that. So, why do you have your house, your car, and your bank account? It is a test of your spirituality. How are you doing? That is the issue. You don't need it because God is going to take care of you. God is testing the legitimacy of your spiritual claim by your possessions. I believe that the best revealer of true spirituality is money. And that is the Lord's intention—how we handle luxury (Matt. 6:19-24) and how we handle necessity (Matt. 6:25-34).

A careful reading of the Bible will reveal that rich people are condemned. But they are never condemned for their riches, only for the misuse of them. We live in a society where we have riches. May God help us not to misuse them. Poor people are also condemned in the Bible, not because they are poor but because they question God's equity and love. Being poor is a test of trust, as is being rich. When you have it, you trust in it; when you don't have it, maybe you fail to trust God. Possessions and money are a spiritual test.

I hope you will examine yourself as to your attitude toward luxuries and necessities. Proverbs 30:8b-9 says, "Give me neither poverty nor riches, but give me only my daily bread. Otherwise, I may have too much and disown you and say, 'Who is the Lord?' Or I may become poor and steal, and so dishonor the name of my God" (NIV*). It is a test whether you have wealth or not. The one who has it is tempted not to trust God; the one who doesn't have it is tempted to dishonor His name.

Focusing on the Facts

1. What are the temptations that affect both the poor and the rich? What is the proper perspective for both of these groups of people (see p. 45)?
2. What is the test that money allows every Christian to take (see p. 46)?
3. What is the major problem that has been revealed as a result of our incredible affluence? Why is it a problem (see pp. 46-47)?
4. Explain the trap that man has fallen into as a result of the technology of the world (see p. 47).
5. Why do many Christians seek after material possessions rather than the things of God (see p. 47)?
6. On what three things is our contentment with God founded (see pp. 49-52)?
7. How much does God own? Support your answer (see p. 49).
8. What is the danger when you think that you own something (see p. 49)?
9. What is the legacy that has been handed down to us from history (see p. 50)?
10. How much does God control? Support your answer (see pp. 51-52).
11. Why was Daniel so relaxed and unafraid when he was in the lions' den (see p. 52)?
12. Why does God own everything and control everything (see p. 52)?
13. What does the Christian life consist of (see p. 54)?
14. How should the Christian use what God has given him (see pp. 54-55)?
15. What is a major issue that faces Christianity today? Explain (see pp. 55-56).
16. Why don't you need the money and possessions you presently have (see p. 57)?

*New International Version.

17. Why are both the rich and the poor alike condemned in the Bible (see p. 57)?

(see p. 57)

Pondering the Principles

1. Have you ever had anything stolen? Have you ever had your car hit by someone when you were not at fault? Have you ever been struck by some tragedy, such as losing your house or your business? How did you respond? How should you have responded? Make a list of the things you have learned about the fact of God's ownership of everything. How can you apply these things to those things that are presently in your possession? What necessary changes do you need to make in regard to your perspective of these things? If you are still holding onto something as if it were yours, take time right now to give it back to God, recognizing His ownership. Thank Him that He has seen fit to bless you with it.

2. Read Philippians 4:6-19. Why does Paul say you should be anxious for nothing? What should be our priority as Christians? What kind of example does Paul provide for us? Why was Paul content? What were the "all things" he could do through Christ? According to verse 19, what happens to those who risk their future well-being by giving of their possessions to meet a need? What needs are you aware of that exist presently in the Body of Christ? Do you have the resources to meet one of those needs? If so, is there anything that should prevent you from meeting that need? Ask God to give you the wisdom to best employ the resources He has given you to meet that need. Then thank Him for the privilege.

3. Are you content with what God has blessed you with, or do you seek to possess more things? What is wrong with this kind of attitude? According to Matthew 6:20-21, where do you find true contentment? Would you covenant with God right now to begin to stockpile your treasures in the heavenly vault and not the earthly one?

4
Overcoming Financial Worry— Part 1

Outline

Introduction
A. The Expression of Worry
   1. Its danger
   2. Its definition
B. The Essentials of Worry
C. The Executors of Worry
   1. Their reasons
   2. Their redirection

Review

Lesson
I. The General Principle
   A. The Command
   B. The Concern
   C. The Connection
   D. The Conditions
      1. The implications of the surroundings
         a) In the present
         b) In the past
      2. The impact of the statement
   E. The Containment
II. The Guiding Protection
   A. Unnecessary Because of Your Faith
      1. The illustrations
         a) Food
            (1) His inclusive provision
               (a) Job 38:41*a*
               (b) Psalm 147:9*b*
            (2) Your important position
            (3) Man's idle practice

   (*a*) A bird's earthly instinct
   (*b*) A Christian's eternal inheritance
 b) The future
  (1) The amount
  (2) The addition
   (*a*) The exercise of obsession
   (*b*) The end of obedience
 c) Fashion
  (1) The anxiety
  (2) The analogy
   (*a*) A wild flower's character
    i) Encompassing beauty
    ii) Essential beauty
    iii) Effortless beauty
   (*b*) Solomon's contrast
  (3) The argument

Introduction

In order that you might have the context for this lesson, let's read Matthew 6:25-34: "Therefore, I say unto you, Be not anxious for your life, what ye shall eat, or what ye shall drink; nor yet for your body, what ye shall put on. Is not the life more than food and the body than raiment? Behold the fowls of the air; for they sow not, neither do they reap, nor gather into barns, yet your heavenly Father feedeth them. Are ye not much better than they? Which of you by being anxious can add one cubit unto his stature? And why are ye anxious for raiment? Consider the lilies of the field, how they grow; they toil not, neither do they spin, and yet I say unto you that even Solomon, in all his glory, was not arrayed like one of these. Wherefore, if God so clothe the grass of the field, which today is, and tomorrow is cast into the oven, shall he not much more clothe you, O ye of little faith? Therefore, be not anxious saying, What shall we eat? or, What shall we drink? or, With what shall we be clothed? For after all these things do the Gentiles seek. For your heavenly Father knoweth that ye have need of all these things. But seek ye first the kingdom of God, and his righteousness, and all these things shall be added unto you. Be, therefore, not anxious about tomorrow; for tomorrow will be anxious for the things of itself. Sufficient unto the day is its own evil."

There is an often-repeated phrase in this passage that becomes the theme: "Be not anxious." It appears three times. *Anxious* is a word that simply means "to worry." "Don't worry" is the heart and soul of the passage. The Lord is calling for us to cease from worrying.

A. The Expression of Worry

1. Its danger

All of us have to admit that worry is a part of life. It is a favorite pastime for most people. It occupies their thinking for a great portion of their day. However, worry is a very dangerous thing—it takes a severe toll on people. But far beyond its psychological effect is the fact that the Bible says that worry is a sin for a child of God. Worry is the equivalent of saying, "God, I know You mean well by what You say, but I'm just not sure You can pull it off." Worry is the sin of distrusting the promise and the providence of God—yet we do it all the time.

William Inge said, "Worry is interest paid on trouble before it is due." A.S. Roche said, "Worry is a thin stream of fear trickling through the mind. If encouraged, it cuts a channel into which all other thoughts are drained." William Ward put it this way: "Worry is faith in the negative, trust in the unpleasant, assurance of disaster and belief in defeat . . . worry is wasting today's time to clutter up tomorrow's opportunities with yesterday's troubles."

I saw an interesting connection with worry in an article I read from the Bureau of Standards in Washington D.C. It was a little feature about the composite element of fog. A dense fog that covers a seven-city-block area one hundred feet deep is composed of less than one glass of water divided into sixty thousand million drops. Not much is there but it can cripple an entire city. I think that is a good illustration of worry.

2. Its definition

The English word *worry* comes from an old German root *wurgen*. Interestingly enough, it means "to choke" or "to strangle." Worry came to mean mental strangulation—harassment from anxiety.

B. The Essentials of Worry

Worry is simply the expression of human sinfulness. We don't worry about anything as much as we worry about the basics of life. We are not different from the people to whom Jesus spoke. They worried about what they were going to eat, drink, and put on their bodies (v. 25). They were worried about the basics. If you want to legitimize your worry, there is no better way than to say, "Well, after all, I'm not worrying about extravagant things; I'm just worrying about my next meal, a glass of water, and something to wear." But that is forbidden for the Christian because it is sinful and foolish. There is no reason for us to worry about the basic commodities of life because that is the Lord's area.

As you read through the Sermon on the Mount, through the gospels, and through the epistles (the commentary on the gospels), one thing you learn is that God does not want His children preoccupied with the mundane, passing things of the earth. He wants us to set our affection not on things of the earth, but on things above. He wants us to lay up our treasure in heaven and to seek first the kingdom of God. In order to free us to do that He says, "Don't worry about the basics; I'll take care of that." A basic principle of spiritual life is that we are not earth-bound people. We give the basics to God, and we are free to live in the heavenlies. How foolish it is to be worried about material things! But that is precisely what people worry about.

C. The Executors of Worry

1. Their reasons

Now, He could be talking about rich people—the same people who have all the luxuries (vv. 19-24) are also worried about the necessities (vv. 25-34). Rich people worry about necessities; that's why they stockpile all their money as a hedge against the future. They stash it away so that in case everything falls apart, they will still be able to have it all. Poor people worry about necessities in a little different way—they just can't do anything specific to relieve their worry. At least rich people can stockpile. I think the Lord is primarily directing this passage to poor people, but it encompasses the rich because anybody can worry about having the necessities of life.

There are people in our own society who have all they need and yet are worried about running out. They are worried about what will happen in the future—they won't have enough resources, enough clothing, enough food, enough to drink, or enough shelter. In fear they begin to hedge against the future. Expressing no trust, they try to determine their own destiny apart from God. Even Christians do this. So, He could be referring to the rich, but primarily I think He is talking about the person who has no resources for the future and is totally dependent on today, with tomorrow fulfilling itself.

2. Their redirection

You say, "Why, poor people *should* worry. How do they know where their next meal is going to come from? How do they know they will have it in the morning? How do they know they are going to have shelter and clothes?" But our Lord precisely says that you are not to worry about that. You are not to stash your luxuries as a hedge against the future, and you are not to use for yourself what God has given you for the accomplishment of His purposes (vv. 19-24). Nor are you to have anxiety in your heart for tomorrow's needs even if you have nothing (vv. 25-34).

Review

Now here is some background on the text. Throughout the Sermon on the Mount the Lord was laying down a standard that was uncommon in His day and far beyond the religion of Judaism. He gave them a new standard that was really a reiteration of the older, divine standard. He gave them the divine standard regarding themselves, regarding the world, regarding God's law, regarding moral issues, regarding religious worship, and in these verses regarding their money and possessions. Throughout the Sermon on the Mount the Lord was giving the categories where God speaks to particular issues. God has something to say about your attitudes, something about your commitment to the Word of God, something about your religious activity, something about your moral values, something about your money, something about your possessions, and something about your prayer life. In other words, He sweeps through all of the dimensions of life in this great sermon. At this point we are touching particularly on the necessities of life in Matthew 6:25-34.

Someone might say, "Well, I read verses 19-24, and it says, 'Don't lay up for yourselves treasures on earth. Just lay it up in heaven—don't serve money, serve God.'" But someone else might say, "But what about the future? If I don't stash a lot of it away in this changing world, how do I know if I'm going to have food and drink in the future? How do I know if I'm going to have clothes for myself and my family? How do I know if I'm going to have a shelter?" I believe in wise planning, but if you are having trouble trusting in the future, the Lord says, "Don't worry about that." It's fine to save for the future, it's fine to plan for the future, but it's wrong to worry about those plans, because God will take care of them. If you have a choice between using money now for one of God's purposes and saving it for the unknown future based on your own feeling, then to keep it for the future is to disobey the moment.

Now these are general principles that you will have to apply. We may have treasure, which we are free to lay up in heaven when we don't worry about the necessities of life.

Lesson

I. THE GENERAL PRINCIPLE (v. 25)

A. The Command

"Therefore, I say unto you, Be not anxious."

This phrase is repeated in verse 31, "Be not anxious," and verse 34, "Be . . . not anxious." That is the all-inclusive theme of the passage. In the Greek it simply means "don't worry." In verse 25 the Greek tense is unique and means "stop worrying." It is different in verse 31: "Don't start worrying." So, if you are worrying, quit; if you haven't started, don't.

B. The Concern

"For your life."

The Greek word for "life" is *psuchē*. It has to do with the fullness of earthly, physical, external life. Don't be anxious about this temporal, external, physical, earthly world—the eating, drinking, clothing, and housing. If you have already started, then stop worrying about it.

C. The Connection

"Therefore."

The word "therefore" is there to take us backwards to the three principles in verses 19-24. First of all, He said that earthly treasures corrupt. Then He said that yearning for earthly treasures blinds your spiritual vision. Third, He said that you must make a choice between God and money. To sum it all up, since earthly treasures corrupt you, since earthly treasures tend to blind your spiritual vision, and since earthly treasures tend to draw you away from serving God, therefore, don't worry about those kinds of things. That should not be your preoccupation. You say, "Well, can't we at least worry about the basics, if not the luxuries?" Not at all. If you are a child of God you have a single goal (treasure in heaven), you have a single vision (you see God's purposes), and you have a single Master (you serve God, not money). Therefore, you cannot become preoccupied with the things of this world.

D. The Conditions

"What ye shall eat, or what ye shall drink; nor yet for your body, what ye shall put on."

1. The implications of the surroundings

   a) In the present

   Now, in our society we might think that is a little bit obscure. We say, "I don't worry about that. There's a supermarket on every block. We've got so much water in our house we never think about it. What do you mean, worry about water? Who worries about that?" And then some prophet of doom comes along and says we're running out of food and water in America, and maybe we do worry a little.

   b) In the past

   But if you were living in Palestine at Jesus' time, you might have been a little more concerned. There were times when the snows didn't come to the mountains, and as a result the streams didn't run. In the burning summer heat the streams would dry up, and there would be no water. There were also times when the crops didn't come through because a plague of locusts ate them. When the crops didn't come through there was famine in the land. When there was famine in the land there was also no income. When there was no income in the land there could be no purchase of clothing. So, there were none of the real resources that people needed to live by.

2. The impact of the statement

   These words of our Lord are powerful, spoken in the context of that time. When He said, "Don't you ever bother to worry about what you're going to eat, drink, and wear," to those people on the edge of the parched desert, who were totally dependent upon the natural resources, it must have been a shocking statement. Certainly that is an indictment of our own worry about those kinds of things. Our Lord recognizes that man, in his covetousness, tends to devote his whole life to caring for the externals— his food, his house, his clothes, and so on.

E. The Containment

"Is not the life [Gk., *psuchē*, 'the fullness of physical life']
more than food and the body than raiment?"

Is that all there is in life? Most people in our world are totally
consumed with the body—decorate it, fix it up, clothe it, take
care of it, put it in a nice car, send it off to a nice house, stuff
it full of nice food, sit it in a nice comfortable chair, hang a
bunch of jewelry all over it, take it out on a boat, let it swim,
teach it to ski, take it on a cruise. That is the way most people
live. Isn't life more than that? The body isn't the end of
everything. Life is not contained in this body; life is contained
in the very nature of God. I live not because my body lives,
but because God gives my body life. Life is more than the
body, more than food, more than clothes. You will never
convince people in our society of that, but it's true.

II. THE GUIDING PROTECTION (vv. 26-32, 34)

Jesus gives three reasons why you shouldn't worry. One, it is
unnecessary because of your Father; two, it is uncharacteristic
because of your faith; and three, it is unwise because of your
future.

A. Unnecessary Because of Your Father (vv. 26-30)

It is unnecessary to worry about finances, the basics of life,
and what you eat or drink or wear because of your Father.
Have you forgotten who your Father is? For example, my
children don't worry about where they are going to get their
next meal. They don't worry about whether they are going to
have clothes, a bed, or something to drink. That never enters
their minds because they know enough about their father to
know he provides for them. And believe me, I don't come
close to being as faithful as God. Yet how often we fail to
believe that God is going to provide for us! Anxiety is foolish.

1. The illustrations

The Lord gives three illustrations: one from food, one
from the future, and one from fashion.

a) Food (v. 26)

"Behold the fowls of the air; for they sow not, neither
do they reap, nor gather into barns, yet your heavenly Father feedeth them. Are ye not much better
than they?"

(1) His inclusive provision (v. 26*a*)

"Behold the fowls of the air."

I see the Lord standing on the hillside up in Galilee looking down over that beautiful north end of the sea, the breeze rippling across the water, the sun bright in the sky. The people were all gathered at His feet. It was a lovely time of the year and a lovely place to be. As He was speaking to them, some birds might have flown across the sky. A. Parmalee has said that the north part of the area of Galilee is the crossroads of bird migration. Jesus probably saw them fly by.

Every bird that lives in this world lives because God gave it life. If God gives life to a bird, He doesn't say, "I have given you life; now you figure out how to keep it." Birds don't get together and say, "We have got to come up with a strategy to keep ourselves alive." Birds have no self-consciousness, no cognitive processes, no ability to reason. But God has planted within birds something called instinct, so that they have a divine capacity to find what is necessary to live. God doesn't just create life; He also sustains life.

(*a*) Job 38:41*a*—"Who provideth for the raven his prey? When his young ones cry unto God." In other words, the little birds actually look to God the Creator. It is God the Creator who gave the mother the instinct to bring food. It is God the Creator who gave the mother the instinct to build the nest and to migrate to a new area at an exact and precise time.

(*b*) Psalm 147:9*b*—"To the young ravens which cry," He gives food. God feeds the birds through the process of their own instinct, which the Bible calls "crying out to God." Now, if God is going to take care of irrational birds who cry out to Him through their instinct, is not God going to take care of His own children?

(2) Your important position (v. 26*c*)

"Are ye not much better than they?"

Arthur Pink said, "Here we may see how the

irrational creatures, made subject to vanity by the sin of man, come nearer to their first estate and better observe the order of nature in their creation than man does, for they seek only for that which God has provided for them, and when they receive it, they are content . . . this solemnly demonstrates that man is more corrupt than other creatures, more vile and base than are the brute beasts." God takes care of birds; don't you think He will take care of you?

(3) Man's idle practice (v. 26*b*)

"For they sow not, neither do they reap, nor gather into barns, yet your heavenly Father feedeth them."

(*a*) A bird's earthly instinct

This is not an excuse for idleness. Some bird says, "I'm just going to stand out there on the edge of a tree with my mouth open." Now, it never rains worms. God feeds birds through an instinct that tells them where to find that food, and they work for it. They are busy searching, gobbling up little insects and worms, preparing their nests, caring for their young, teaching them to fly, pushing them out of the nest at the right time, migrating with the seasons, and so on. All this work has to be done if they are going to eat, and yet they do it by instinct and never overdo it. They don't say, "I'm going to build bigger nests. I'm going to store more worms. I'm going to say to myself, 'Bird—eat, drink, and be merry.' " They work within the framework of God's design for them, and they never overindulge themselves. Birds get fat only when people put them in cages.

Men are the ones who have enough and continually stockpile and hoard. They ignore God's priorities and promises and ultimately forfeit the carefree heart. The birds don't worry about where they are going to find their food, they just fly till they find it—and God provides it. Birds have no reason to worry, and if *they* don't, what are you worrying for?

(b) A Christian's eternal inheritance

Are you not much better than a bird? No bird was ever created in the image of Christ, no bird was ever made in the image of God, no bird was ever designed to be a joint heir with Jesus Christ throughout eternity, and no bird was ever prepared a place in heaven in the Father's house. If God sustains the life of a bird, don't you think He will take care of you? Life is a gift from God. If God gives you the greater gift, which is life, don't you think He will give you the lesser gift, which is the sustaining of that life by food? Of course, so don't worry about it.

If God speaks to me about the resources that I am keeping for the future and says, "John, I want you to do this certain thing with all of those resources," then I don't have any right to say, "But Lord, if I do that, what am I going to do for tomorrow? I won't have any food or clothes for my children." If God asks for this now, it becomes His responsibility to feed me tomorrow—and He will. If He gave me the greater gift of life, will He not give me the lesser gift (food) to sustain that life? Like a bird, I have to work because God has designed that man should earn his bread by the sweat of his brow (Gen. 3:19). If I don't work, then I don't eat (2 Thess. 3:10).

Just as God provides for the bird through its instinct, so God provides for man through his effort. If God gives me the gift of life then He will sustain me. Martin Luther said, "God . . . wants nothing to do with the lazy, gluttonous bellies who are neither concerned nor busy: they act as if they just had to sit and wait for Him to drop a roasted goose into their mouth." Jesus is not saying to do nothing, but through my effort God will provide.

70

Are We Running Out of Food?

People say, "We are running out of resources." There is much food in this world, because God is always in the business of abundance. This world hasn't seen anything yet; wait until we get to the Millennium! So, you are not to worry about whether God can handle the current crisis.

I read an article from the United States Department of Agriculture that I thought was interesting. These are the responses to two questions asked:

- Question #1—"Is the world's food supply large enough to meet everyone's minimum needs?"
- Answer #1—"The world has more than enough food to feed every man, woman, and child in it. If the world's food supply had been evenly divided and distributed among the world's population for the last 18 years, each person would have received more than the *minimum* number of calories. From 1960 to the present, world food grain production never dropped below 103 percent of the minimum requirements and averaged 108 percent between 1973 and 1977.

"Thus, if a system existed today to distribute grains equitably, the world's 4 billion people would have available about one-fifth more grain per person than the 2.7 billion people had 25 years ago."

- Question #2—"Hasn't the amount of food produced per person been dropping in the developing countries of the world over the last 25 years?"
- Answer #2—"This is a common misconception. Food production in the developing countries has been increasing. . . .

"World per capita food production declined only twice in the last 25 years—in 1972 and 1974. . . . Production of grain, the primary food for most of the world's people, rose from 290 kilograms per person during the early 1950's to an average of 360 kilograms during the past five years, about a 25-percent increase."

There is more food than there has ever been. As far as potential food production is concerned, the world could feed every single person in it on the standard of the U.S. consumption by using less than 10 percent of the agricultural land available on the earth and using more of its other resources. When God says that He will provide, He means

He will provide.

You say, "Why don't some people have anything to eat?" I don't think it's because God doesn't provide; I think it's because they are not His children and He has no obligation to them. Take India, for example. India has plenty of food to feed its people, but there is starvation there. They allow sacred cows to eat 20 percent of all their food, and the rodents that they believe are reincarnations of their ancestors eat 15 percent. That is a total of 35 percent of their food. It is not that they don't have the resources; they just don't have the spiritual connection to God that puts them in the place of blessing. Their religion destroys them.

There is plenty of food. God will provide as we are faithful to believe His Word. You should never worry about your food. That is unnecessary because of your Father.

b) The future (v. 27)

"Which of you by being anxious can add one cubit unto his stature?"

(1) The amount

A cubit was the distance from the elbow to the tips of the fingers—about eighteen inches.

(2) The addition

The verse says, "Which of you by being anxious [worrying] can add one cubit unto his stature?" Now, nobody would want to add a foot and a half to his stature. There is a better way to translate the word "stature." The Greek word is *hēlikia* and is used sometimes to mean "span of life." He is really saying, "Which of you by worrying can lengthen your life?" Not only will you not lengthen your life by worrying, but you will probably shorten it.

(a) The exercise of obsession

We live in a day when people are in a panic to lengthen their lives. We are concerned about vitamins, health spas, and exercise. We are cultic about the "body beautiful." I believe God has determined the times of the nations and bounded the life of a man—He has designed how long we live. You say, "Are you saying exercise is useless?" No, as long

72

as I'm going to live I would like to increase the quality of my life. If I exercise I function better, my brain works better, and I'm happier and in control. But I'm not going to kid myself that by running down the street everyday I'm going to force God to let me live longer. Our world has missed the point. We spend a literal fortune joining spas, buying vitamins by the ton, visiting every doctor in sight to get a physical, following every special diet conceivable, and all we want to do is lengthen life. We don't want to die; we want to live longer and longer. We will only make ourselves miserable in the process.

(b) The end of obedience

Charles Mayo of the Mayo Clinic said, "Worry affects the circulation, the heart, the glands, the whole nervous system. I have never known a man to die of overwork, but many who died of worry." You can worry yourself to death but you will never worry yourself to life—and yet that is what people do. When you worry about how long you are going to live and how to add years onto your life, you are distrusting God. That is foolish because if you give Him your life and are obedient to Him, He will give you the fullness of days.

I believe that the gift of life is given because God wants you to live for spiritual reasons. In the Old Testament, it was in response to obedience that God promised to give long life. As long as we live a righteous life, there is a reason for us to be alive. God bounds our life by His sovereign decree, and He wants us to live life to its fullest. Exercise and health help because we are kept alert and alive to the limits of our capacity while we are living out our span. But we can't worry ourselves into a longer life. We will experience life to the fullest if we're obedient to God.

The first point is this: Worry is unnecessary because of your Father. The first illustration of that is food,

73

and the second is the future or the length of life. The third is:

c) Fashion (vv. 28-30a)

Some people live for clothes. The most important place in their whole world is the closet.

(1) The anxiety (v. 28a)

"And why are ye anxious for raiment?"

In those times, if you were really poor you did not have any resources. In our society we worry more about the fact that what we wear isn't really what is in style. People live for clothes. They manifest a carnal, selfish, worldly, materialistic care for clothes. It isn't so much that they are afraid they will have nothing to wear—it is that they are afraid they won't be able to look their best. Lusting after costly clothes is a sin in our society.

Whenever I walk through a shopping mall, I can't believe how much stuff is hanging on those racks. I don't know how those stores can sustain the inventory. We have made a god out of fashion. We sinfully indulge in a money-mad spending spree to buy ourselves things to drape over the body that have nothing to do with the beauty of character. First Peter 3:3-4a says, "Let it not be that outward adorning of braiding the hair, and of wearing of gold, or of putting on of apparel, but let it be the hidden man of the heart." We worry that we don't have enough and don't look good enough, when the Lord Jesus, who owned only what He wore on His back, was the loveliest who ever lived.

(2) The analogy (vv. 28b-29)

(a) A wild flower's character (v. 28b)

i) Encompassing beauty

"Consider the lilies of the field."

What are the field lilies? They were most likely no particular flower at all. "Field lilies" is just a general term for all of the wild flowers that graced the rolling hills of Galilee. There were many—the anem-

74

ones, the gladioli, the irises, the narcissus, and the little cap lilies. These flowers were all over those hillsides. They even had what I think might be the prettiest of all—little scarlet-colored poppies that would grow for just a brief season. But the hillsides of Galilee at the right time of year would be dotted with the brightness of all these lovely flowers. There is such a wondrous beauty about a flower. When Christ said to look at the field lilies, I'm sure He swept His arm to indicate the flowers.

ii) Essential beauty

"They toil not, neither do they spin."

Flowers don't make fancy thread and hang it all over themselves and say, "I've been scarlet for two days; I think I would like to be blue tomorrow."

Recently, I read about a business where you go for a consultation as to what colors you should wear. They give you a chart that shows you what bracket you belong in. You can then buy all of the right colors that emphasize your lips and your eyes and your hair.

Look at the little flowers in the field. They don't bother to spin and toil—there is a free and easy beauty about them. You can take the most glorious material or the most beautiful thing that was ever made for the greatest monarch, like Solomon, put it under a microscope, and it will look like sackcloth. But if you take the petal of a flower and put it under a microscope, you will see the difference. I have seen plastic flowers, I have seen silk flowers, and I have seen paper flowers, but I have never seen anything come close to the beauty of the petal of a real flower. There is a texture and form and design and substance and color that man with all of his ingenuity cannot even touch.

iii) Effortless beauty

"How they grow."

They grow easily, freely, gorgeously— effortlessly they flourish. The stupidity of pride in dress is an indictment of our day. We spend so much time and effort. And they keep changing the fashions on us all the time in order to keep us preoccupied. You cannot go into a clothing store or department store without its literally being an assault on your mind and eyes. It is an enticement to the lust to have and possess. And when you have it all on and have dressed yourself up the best you can, you are not even close to a flower. Now, I am not saying one should look seedy and tacky—that is a negative distraction that will make people think you don't care for yourself. But you can lose your sense of perspective and be that one step short of the real beauty that only God can give.

(b) Solomon's contrast (v. 29)

"And yet I say unto you that even Solomon, in all his glory, was not arrayed like one of these."

Even Solomon, the greatest, richest, and wisest, had no garment that could approximate the texture, the fragile beauty, and the incredible design of a flower. When you have done all you can to yourself, you still can't do what God can do with one little tiny flower. Why do you spend such an effort for such a result?

(3) The argument (v. 30a)

"Wherefore, if God so clothe the grass of the field [all the flowers and the grass], which today is, and tomorrow is cast into the oven, shall he not much more clothe you?"

Do you know what they used to do with that old grass? The women in that part of the world cooked upon little hearths. They had a thick clay oven with a little door, which could be placed on top of the fire. They would let the fire heat the oven until it would heat the inside. Then they could open the door and put in whatever they wanted to cook. But if the fire had grown low or they were in a hurry and couldn't wait for the inside to heat up, they would start a fire on the inside of that little oven. Historians tell us that they would go into the field and find dried grass that had become brittle and flowers that had died. They would then gather the little stalks of the flowers and grass to put into the oven in order to start a fire on the inside that would help the fire coming from the outside evenly warm the oven.

Don't worry about what you wear, don't worry about how long you live, don't worry about what you're going to eat and drink—God takes care of all that. A God who would lavish such beauty on a flower will lavish the necessary clothing on one who is His eternal child.

The Lord will give you food and clothing, He will determine the length of your life and sustain it—that is very tangible. You have no grounds for financial worry if your heart is right. The key is: "But seek ye first the kingdom of God, and his righteousness, and all these things shall be added unto you" (Matt. 6:33). The key is to put your heart and your treasure in heaven, and God will take care of all the earthly things. I don't want to give one minute of the day to thinking about physical, mundane, earthly things.

An old poem expresses this lesson simply:

> Said the wild flower to the sparrow:
> "I should really like to know
> Why these anxious human beings
> Rush about and worry so."
>
> Said the sparrow to the wild flower:
> "Friend I think that it must be
> That they have no heavenly Father,
> Such as cares for you and me."

We ought to learn from the birds and the flowers how to live life. The sum of this is clear: Don't worry—it is unnecessary because of your Father.

Focusing on the Facts

1. What is the theme of Matthew 6:25-34 (see p. 61)?
2. Why is worry a sin for a child of God (see p. 62)?
3. What does the root of the word *worry* mean? What meaning did that eventually have (see p. 62)?
4. What do people worry about more than anything else? Why does God not want the Christian to worry about these things (see pp. 62-63)?
5. Why do rich people worry about the necessities of life? Why do poor people worry about necessities (see p. 63)?
6. Why is it wrong to save money for the future when there is an opportunity to use it now for one of God's purposes (see pp. 64-65)?
7. What kind of connection does the word *therefore* make at the beginning of Matthew 6:25? What should your preoccupation be (see pp. 65-66)?
8. Why did the people of Palestine have cause to worry about their food, water, and clothing (see p. 66)?
9. Why is life more than just our physical bodies (see p. 67)?
10. Why shouldn't a Christian worry? List the three reasons (see p. 67).
11. What are the three aspects of life that our Lord uses to illustrate the fact that worry is unnecessary (see p. 67)?
12. How does God sustain the life of a bird? What does the fact that God sustains the life of a bird have to do with the life of humans (see pp. 68-69)?
13. What do birds do in order to eat? Why don't the birds worry about their effort in obtaining food (see p. 69)?
14. What Scripture passages show that man is to work in order to obtain his food? How does God provide food for us (see p. 70)?
15. Why isn't the world running out of food? Support your answer (see p. 71).
16. Why do so many people in the world lack the necessary amount of food to eat (see p. 72)?
17. What is the best way to translate the word "stature" in Matthew 6:27? Given this translation, what does the verse mean (see p. 72)?
18. What is one of the main reasons that people in the world exercise? What should be the true motive behind exercise (see pp. 72-73)?
19. What is revealed about your relationship to God when you worry about the length of your life? What is it that will ultimately bring about a long and full life (see p. 73)?
20. What is the attitude that God wants in regard to the adornment of ourselves (see p. 74)?

21. What were the field lilies that Jesus referred to in Matthew 6:28? Why did He use them as an illustration (see pp. 74-75)?
22. Why was the old grass thrown into the oven (see pp. 76-77)?
23. What is the key verse of Matthew 6:25-34? Why (see p. 77)?

Pondering the Principles

1. Are worry and anxiety a part of your daily life? Make a list of the various things you worry about. How many of them come under the category of necessities— food, drink, clothing, and shelter? Is your worry over these things mainly concerned with the present or the future? According to Matthew 6:33 these things are not your concern, but God's. What are you to be preoccupied with? How much of the day is your mind set on heavenly things? In order to begin to alleviate your anxiety, memorize the simple priority and promise that Jesus gives you in Matthew 6:33: "But seek ye first the kingdom of God, and his righteousness, and all these things shall be added unto you."

2. God is our Father. Perhaps you are a parent. Even if you are not, you might have some idea of the love a parent has for his children. List as many things as you can think of that a parent does for his children. How many of these things has God done for you? What things has God done for you that are not even on this list? What does this tell you about God's special love for you as His child? How does this relate to your anxiety? Take this time to thank God for His love and care for you. Then begin to turn your anxiety over to Him by committing into His care one of the things from the list in question 1.

3. Look up Genesis 3:19 and 2 Thessalonians 3:10. How has God designed for man to earn his food? What happens if he doesn't follow God's design? God will provide for man just like He does for the birds if man will only follow His design. Look up the following verses: Leviticus 26:3-5; Deuteronomy 5:32-33; 8:1; Jeremiah 38:20; John 12:26. What does God do for those who are obedient to Him? How do these verses relate to your worry over necessities? Instead of worrying, what should you be doing? Make it a point to begin to seek His kingdom and His righteousness by being obedient.

5
Overcoming Financial Worry—
Part 2

Outline

Introduction
A. The Emerging Perspective
    1. The scarcity
    2. The solution
B. The Biblical Perspective
    1. The luxuries
       a) Eternal significance
       b) Clear sight
       c) Undivided service
    2. The necessities

Review
  I. The General Principle
 II. The Guiding Protection
A. Unnecessary Because of Your Father
    1. The illustrations
       a) Food
       b) The future
       c) Fashion

Lesson
    2. The indictment
       a) The representatives of worry
       b) The results of worry
          (1) Worry strikes out at God
          (2) Worry disbelieves Scripture
          (3) Worry is mastered by circumstances
          (4) Worry distrusts God
B. Uncharacteristic Because of Your Faith
    1. The ignorance of Gentiles
       a) Living without divine resources

      b) Living in fear
      c) Living like the world
         (1) Expressions of the Christian faith
            (*a*) Philippians 4:6
            (*b*) John 17:15
            (*c*) Romans 12:2*a*
         (2) Examinations for Christian faithfulness
    2. The knowledge of God
  C. Unwise Because of Your Future
    1. Worries of tomorrow
    2. Grace for today
      a) Sustaining His perfection
      b) Staying in port
III. The Guaranteed Promise
  A. The Contrast
  B. The Concern
    1. "The kingdom of God"
      a) Conversion
      b) Commitment
      c) Coming again
    2. "And his righteousness"
  C. The Care

Introduction

The instruction from the Sermon on the Mount preached by our Lord Jesus Christ is practical and touches us right where we live. The heart of the matter to which Jesus speaks in Matthew 6:25-34 is the issue of materialism—worrying about our finances, worrying about our lives, worrying about our earthly existence, and worrying about the necessities of life. Three times the Lord gives the injunction in this passage that we are not to worry. Such anxiety, fear, and worry have absolutely no place in the life of a Christian. Of course this is a marked antithesis to everything we know in our own world. The materialistic world in which we live is totally preoccupied with material possessions. Life begins and ends with the things that people possess. Scripture says the exact opposite: "A man's life consisteth not in the abundance of the things which he possesseth" (Luke 12:15*b*). And yet the heart of the matter, even in our own country, is that most people live for nothing more and nothing less than all the possessions they can possibly grasp to feed their determined life-style. But the whole thing may be crumbling before their very eyes because America cannot sustain this constant economic overindulgence, overconsumption, and overproduction that it is currently experiencing.

A. The Emerging Perspective

An interesting book entitled *The Emerging Order*, written by Jeremy Rifkin and Ted Howard, says that we cannot continue to overproduce and overconsume and still maintain our current approach to life.

1. The scarcity

For example, they say, "We are nearing the end of an epoch that stretches across half a millennium of history. The age of expansion with faith in unlimited economic growth and the governing truths of science and technology, is about to give way to a new age of scarcity and economic contraction, an age so utterly different from our own that any serious attempt to give form and substance to it all but boggles the mind." In other words, we are a generation of incredible materialists and limited resources.

Rifkin and Howard go on to say, "Emphasis on continuous economic growth is a black hole that has already sucked up a majority of the world's critical non-renewable resources" (New York: Ballantine, 1983). We have overproduction, overconsumption, and a materialistic economic mania that not only destroys the soul but the environment as well.

2. The solution

At the close of their book they offer a solution: The reemergence of the evangelical Christian ethic—an ethic of unselfishness and low consumption. If we don't return to an evangelical ethic we will wind up in a constrictive, totalitarian dictatorship where we will have no freedom.

I wonder if that is still the evangelical Christian ethic. I am not sure that even if we were given the responsibility to pull it off we would still have the commitment to live the ethic. If we want to have an effect on our society, then we are going to have to be distinctively Christian. Unfortunately, we are almost as materialistic as those who are a part of the system around us. We all suffer from the inroads, the temptations, and the power of the materialistic age in which we live. We have all fallen prey to it. So, when somebody outside of Christianity calls for us to be the standard, we should reexamine our own house to make sure we still have what it takes to live that standard.

B. The Biblical Perspective

What is the Christian view of money and possessions? Where do we stand, and what does the Bible teach? What is my perspective to be on the luxuries and necessities of life? Our own Lord Jesus Christ gives the answer to these questions in Matthew 6:19-34— the greatest statement Jesus ever made on the view we must have toward material things. Verses 19-24 deal with our view of luxury. In verses 25-34 He speaks of our view of necessity. So, the Lord touches on that which is beyond what we need and that which we need. He gives us an affirmation of where our commitment is to be.

1. The luxuries

What is to be our perspective on luxury—that which is beyond what we need for the basic necessities? The Lord makes a simple statement in verse 20a: "But lay up for yourselves treasures in heaven." We are to invest in heaven. We are to commit ourselves to placing that which we possess in an eternal investment, not stockpiling it in earthly things because moths, rust, and thieves will destroy it (v. 19). And we are to do this for three reasons:

a) Eternal significance

According to verse 21, our heart should be in heaven. If you put all your treasure in the earth, that is where your heart will be. You will worry about your bank account instead of the kingdom of God. But if you invest all that you have in God's purposes and projects, then your heart will be there as you watch your investment bringing eternal dividends.

b) Clear sight

According to verses 22-23 our spiritual eyes are opened. The Lord says that if you invest in the earth, you pull the shades down on your spiritual eyes and you become blind to spiritual reality. If you invest in eternal things, the shades go up and the light of God floods your heart.

c) Undivided service

The third reason that we are to invest what we have in eternity: That determines that we serve God and not money. It makes our service to God undivided.

So, in dealing with luxury, we need to invest it in eternity and not stockpile it here. Then the heart is where it should be, our spiritual sight is clear, and our service is undivided. You should invest with God magnanimously and generously because you know the eternal has far more consequence than the temporal.

2. The necessities

From this He moves to the necessities of life in verses 25-34. If we are concerned about anything, we are concerned about the basics. In fact, the reason some people stockpile their luxuries in the present is to hedge against not having the necessities in the future. Is this what we should do?

Review

I. THE GENERAL PRINCIPLE (v. 25; see pp. 65-67)

The heart of this passage is reiterated in three statements: "Therefore, I say unto you, Be not anxious. . . . Therefore, be not anxious. . . . Be, therefore, not anxious" (vv. 25a, 31a, 34a). The thrust of this passage is built around those three statements. In the Greek, the first one says, "Stop being anxious." The next two say, "Don't start being anxious." The Greek word for "anxious" is *merimna*, which means "to worry, to fret, to fear, to have anxiety." In fact, in a Greek manuscript found from the first century, there was a list of names of certain Christians in the early church. One name they found was one Titedios Amerimnos. By putting an α (alpha) in front of *merimnos* it means "not to worry," hence his name was Titedios, the man who never worries.

We are not to worry about "what ye shall eat, or what ye shall drink; nor yet for your body, what ye shall put on" (v. 25b). Don't worry about the basics—your food, your drink, and your clothes.

II. THE GUIDING PROTECTION (vv. 26-32, 34)

You say, "That's easy for you to say. On what basis does He say that?" There are three reasons not to worry: it is unnecessary because of your Father, it is uncharacteristic because of your faith, and it is unwise because of your future. First of all, we are not to worry about the basics of life.

A. Unnecessary Because of Your Father (vv. 26-30; see pp. 67-77)

Worry is unnecessary since God is our Father. If your concept of God is right and you see Him as Owner, Controller, and Provider, and beyond that as your loving Father, then you have nothing about which to worry. If He has all things in His control, then He controls those things on the behalf of His children. If you are His child, that should be the end of worry. For example Matthew 7:7-8 says, "Ask, and it shall be given you; seek, and ye shall find; knock, and it shall be opened unto you; for every one that asketh receiveth; and he that seeketh findeth; and to him that knocketh it shall be opened." Now, those two verses have been applied to many things, but the basic issue to which our Lord is speaking is the issue of physical sustenance.

He illustrates that principle in verses 9-10: "Or what man is there of you whom, if his son ask bread, will he give him a stone? Or if he ask a fish, will he give him a serpent?" In other words, you know that in human terms a man is not going to give his son a rock when he asks for a piece of bread, or give him a snake when he asks for a fish. Human fathers give their children what they seek if what they seek is what they need.

Then verse 11 says, "If ye then, being evil, know how to give good gifts unto your children, how much more shall your Father, who is in heaven [He is not evil but absolutely righteous, just, holy, perfect, and good], give good things to them that ask him?" And "good things" speaks first of the necessities of life. If an evil, sinful father knows how to give good things to his children, won't an absolutely holy God know how to give good things to His children?

1. The illustrations (vv. 26-30a; see pp. 66-77)

   a) Food (v. 26; see pp. 67-72)

   Matthew 6:26 says, "Behold the fowls of the air . . . your heavenly Father feedeth them. Are ye not much better than they?" He is your heavenly Father; if He takes care of birds, don't you think He will take care of you? He will supply your food.

   b) The future (v. 27; see pp. 72-74)

   "Which of you by being anxious can add one cubit unto his stature [life span]?" There are people who worry about how long they are going to live because they are afraid of death. Some people don't want to get on an airplane, some people are afraid of diseases—they go from doctor to doctor, from health spa to health spa, from bottle to bottle of pills. They live in constant fear about their lives. What good does that do? Your Father cares for that. All the worry in the world isn't going to add to your life; if anything, it will subtract from it.

c) Fashion (vv. 28-30*a*; see pp. 74-77)

Some of you worry about whether you have enough clothes or the right clothes to fit into the fashions of the day. But when you are all done dressing yourself, you won't be dressed as beautifully as a lily. Why not let God do the dressing? Solomon, the richest man ever, could not make a robe as fine as the petal of a flower.

In other words, God takes care of food, He takes care of life spans, and He takes care of clothing.

Supplies for the Children

God does provide the basics of life—that's the promise. The basis of the promise is that God is our Father. God is a loving Father who supplies for His children.

1. Psalm 34:10—"The young lions do lack, and suffer hunger" (v. 10*a*). There are times when lion cubs hunger, but the mother is unavailable to provide the food. Yet the psalmist says, "But they who seek the Lord shall not lack any good thing" (v. 10*b*). Animals may lack, but God's people will not. God supports His own. That is a repeated biblical truth that you can find all over the pages of Holy Writ. God sustains His people.

2. Philippians 4:19—"But my God shall supply all your need according to his riches in glory by Christ Jesus." There is nothing to worry about. Why would you worry about your life when all of your worry cannot add one day to your life? Why would you be in great distress over having enough food when God, who gave you life, will give you the lesser gift that sustains that life? Why would you worry about having something to wear when the Lord has designed clothing for human beings? You are His children, and He will give you clothing.

3. 1 Peter 5:7—Peter was a worrier. He worried about drowning when he was walking on the water even though the Lord was right there (Matt. 14:29-31). He

worried about what was going to happen to Jesus in the Garden of Gethsemane, so he pulled his sword and tried to fight the Romans (John 18:10). He worried about Jesus being crucified and told Him not to go to the cross (Matt. 16:22). He was a real worrier. But he finally got the message and writes this great truth in 1 Peter 5:7: "Casting all your care upon him; for he careth for you." It took him awhile to learn it, but he did.

So, first of all, our Lord says don't worry—it is unnecessary because of your Father.

Lesson

2. The indictment (v. 30b)

"O ye of little faith?"

If you worry, what kind of faith do you manifest? Little faith; puny faith; inadequate, infinitesimal faith. The sum of an attitude that worries about food and clothes and life span is an attitude of little faith in God.

a) The representatives of worry

The phrase "O ye of little faith" is used four other times in the gospels. For example, it is used in Luke 12:28 when people worry about clothing. It is used in Matthew 8:24-26 when the disciples worry about drowning—they were afraid the Lord was going to let them drown. They said to Him, "How can You sleep when the storm is going to drown us?" In Matthew 14:31 it is used when Peter is worrying about drowning. And it is used in Matthew 16:8 when they are worried about their food. Every time that phrase was used it referred to someone who worried about food, clothes, or life span. And every time, He directed His speaking to the disciples—those who should have known better.

You believe that God can redeem you, save you from sin, break the shackles of Satan, take you from hell to heaven, put you into His kingdom, and give you eternal life, but you just don't think He can get you something to wear and to eat in the next couple of days. That is pretty ridiculous. We can believe God for the bigger gift, and then we stumble and can't believe Him for the lesser one. We believe God is going to take us to heaven when we die, but we don't believe He is going to provide us a meal or take care of the length of our life. The fact that Jesus speaks to His disciples in each case indicates to me that this is a passage geared for believers. He would never say to unbelievers, "O you of little faith;" He would say, "O you of no faith." We have faith; we just don't apply it.

b) The results of worry

(1) Worry strikes out at God

Someone might say, "Worry is a small, trivial sin." No, it is not trivial. I think that much of mental illness and some physical illness is directly related to worry. Worry is devastating. But more important than what worry does to you is what it does to God. When you worry you are saying in effect, "God, I just don't think I can trust You." Worry then strikes a blow at the Word and the person of God.

(2) Worry disbelieves Scripture

To me, worry is a monumental sin because worry disbelieves Scripture. You can say, "I believe in the inerrancy of the Scripture. I believe in verbal, plenary inspiration of every word," and then just live your life worrying. You are saying one thing out of one side of your mouth, and another thing out of the other. Why would you say how much you believe the Bible and then worry about God fulfilling what He says in it?

(3) Worry is mastered by circumstances

Worry means that you are mastered by your circumstances and not the truth of God. Worry misunderstands your position as a child of God. Worry is a devastating sin—a killing, debilitating, self-indulgent, possessive anxiety that says God cannot care for me. That makes God a liar—it ignores His love and His power. I don't understand how people can make the vicissitudes and the trials and the circumstances of life a bigger issue than their salvation. They can believe God to save them from eternal hell, but they can't believe He can help them in this world. It just doesn't make sense!

In Ephesians 1:18-19a Paul prays, "The eyes of your understanding being enlightened; that ye may know what is the hope of his calling, and what the riches of the glory of his inheritance in the saints, and what is the exceeding greatness of his power toward us who believe." You had better go back to Scripture and have your eyes opened again.

(4) Worry distrusts God

If you worry, you are not trusting your heavenly Father. If you don't trust your heavenly Father, the number one cause might be that you don't know Him well enough. If you knew Him, you would trust Him. You had better study the Word of God and find out who He really is and how He has supplied the needs of His people in the past. That will be your confidence for the future. Even those who know God and study the Word worry now and then. This happens when you are not fresh in the Word every day so that God is in your mind. Then Satan moves into that vacuum and makes you worry about something. That is sin. God is worthy of a greater faith than you give Him.

B. Uncharacteristic Because of Your Faith (vv. 31-32)

Worry is unnecessary because of our Father, and it is uncharacteristic because of our faith. He comes right back to the same principle.

1. The ignorance of Gentiles (vv. 31-32a)

"Therefore, be not anxious saying, What shall we eat? or, What shall we drink? or, With what shall we be clothed? For after all these things do the Gentiles seek."

Jesus said that it is uncharacteristic of our faith to act like ungodly people. For us, worry is needless because of God's bounty, senseless because of God's promise, useless because of our impotence to do anything, and faithless because by doing so, we put ourselves in the same category as an unbeliever.

a) Living without divine resources

The word "Gentile" can also be translated "pagan" or "heathen," and means "people without God and Christ." These people worry about this world. That is all they have going for them. They live to grasp and possess because they don't have God to supply for them, to promise them anything—they don't have any divine resource to come to their aid. They have to do it all on their own. They are ignorant of God's supply, so they anxiously and worryingly set their minds on the necessities. But for a Christian, this is senseless and without excuse. It is a serious sin.

b) Living in fear

When heathen people invent gods, inevitably their deities are not the kind they look to in a trusting way. Whenever the nations of the world build their own gods, they are typically the gods of Satan—the demons behind those gods. They are gods of broken promises, gods who lack compassion, gods of fear, gods of dread, gods that have to be appeased, gods that everyone is afraid of—not gods everyone can count on. They are not gods who supply for their people. The people have to supply for themselves, while at the same time appeasing their god with sacrifices or whatever their religion calls for. Since they have vague ideas about the future life, life becomes consumed in the obsession to obtain comforts, wealth, security, and prestige.

c) Living like the world

In the phrase "For after all these things do the Gentiles seek," the word "seek" gives the idea of an emphatic seeking—they are seeking with all their might, totally consumed in material gratification: "Eat, drink, and be merry, for tomorrow we die. Grab all the gusto you can." Now, imagine a child of God's approaching life in this way. It is ludicrous. The nations of the world seek after these things (Luke 12:30). It is unworthy for us to worry.

(1) Expressions of the Christian faith

The Christian faith says that God will supply all my needs—and God can be trusted. To worry about my food or my physical welfare or my clothing is to have a worldly mind.

(a) Philippians 4:6—"Be anxious for nothing, but in everything, by prayer and supplication with thanksgiving, let your requests be made known unto God." Those who do not trust in God's goodness and promise miss the whole point of being a Christian. So many people have empty professions of faith: "We love Christ and we serve God," but they don't believe God for anything. Instead, they worry. They are in the world, and they are like the world.

(b) John 17:15—"I pray not that thou shouldest take them out of the world, but that thou shouldest keep them from the evil."

(c) Romans 12:2a—"And be not conformed to this world."

Jesus is saying that sons of the King do not conduct themselves like the devil's beggars.

(2) Examinations for Christian faithfulness

Ask yourself the question, "Do I face life like a Christian or a pagan?" Said another way, "When things are difficult or the future is insecure, how do I react?" You will find out for yourself how much you trust God. You could sum up the question this way: "Does my Christian faith affect my view of life?" If it doesn't, you are either not a Christian or you have denied the very essence of your faith. Ask yourself this: "Do I always place everything in the context of my faith—every trial, every anticipation of the future, and every present reality?"

2. The knowledge of God (v. 32b)

"For your heavenly Father knoweth that ye have need of all these things."

There is a basic difference between the gods of the heathen and our God. The gods of the heathen are dumb, ignorant, nonexistent—they don't know anything, and they cannot help their people because they don't exist. But our God knows. If you believe that our God loves and

91

cares, believe that He knows. If God knows my life and my needs, then all I need to know is that He cares. If He knows and cares, then I am home free. Your heavenly Father, in contrast to the gods of the pagans, knows that you have need. He not only has the knowledge, but He has the resources and the love to provide. So, what should you worry about? Nothing!

Worry is unnecessary because of your Father, uncharacteristic because of your faith, and:

C. Unwise Because of Your Future (v. 34)

"Be, therefore, not anxious about tomorrow; for tomorrow will be anxious for the things of itself. Sufficient unto the day is its own evil."

The Lord is saying, "Don't worry about the future. The future is going to have its own trouble. Just wait till you get to it." Don't worry about tomorrow. Now, providing for tomorrow is good, but worrying about tomorrow is sin because God is the God of tomorrow just as He is the God of today. Lamentations 3:23a says that His mercies "are new every morning." He feeds you as He fed the children of Israel—just enough manna for the day.

1. Worries of tomorrow

Worry is a tremendous force. Worry will endeavor to defeat you. First, it will endeavor to destroy you today—it will try to make you upset and anxious. But if it loses today, it will take you into the future until it finds something to make you worry about. That is the way worry functions. I am afraid that some people are so committed to the sin of worry they just keep looking to the future until they find something to worry about. The Lord says that you have enough to deal with today. Take the resources of today for the needs of today or you will lose the joy of today.

Lack of joy is a sin, too. Many people lose their joy because of worry for tomorrow, and they miss the victory God gives them today. That is not fair to Him. God gives you a glorious and blissful day today; live in the light and fullness of the joy of that day and use the resources God supplies. Don't push yourself into the future and forfeit the joy of today over some tomorrow that may never happen. Learn this one little statement: Fear is a liar. It will cause you to lose the joy of today. The Lord forbids worrying about tomorrow: "Let tomorrow be for tomorrow, each day has enough trouble for itself."

2. Grace for today

In addition, God gives strength for only one day at a time. He doesn't give me the grace for tomorrow until tomorrow. Many people worry about dying. But when somebody in their family dies, God gives a wonderful grace and peace and sustaining. They can't understand it! They will say to me, "John, you know it's so wonderful how God has sustained me and supported me. I have a normal sorrow, but I feel strength and confidence and a gladness in my heart that this one I love is with the Lord." And that is right, because God gives us grace for the hour that we need that grace. But if you want to worry about the future now, you are going to double your pain without any grace to deal with it. It is better that you should singly endure the trial with the grace to sustain you through it. I refuse to worry about tomorrow or the next day because I don't have any resource. First of all, fear is a liar—I don't know the reality of what will be; and second, I don't want to double my trouble without the resource of God's grace. So, I shoulder the burden of today. As I see God lift the burden and carry it away from me, I can enjoy today and let tomorrow bring its own trouble. I don't cripple myself by worrying about a future that I cannot live in.

a) Sustaining His perfection

When the Bible says, "Jesus Christ, the same yesterday, and today, and forever" (Heb. 13:8), it means He will be doing the same thing tomorrow that He was doing yesterday. If you have any question about the future, look at the past. Did He sustain you then? He will sustain you in the future. There is no past, present, or future with Him. Worry is forbidden.

John Stott has said, "To become preoccupied with material things in such a way that they engross our attention, absorb our energy and burden us with anxiety is incompatible with both Christian faith and common sense. It is distrustful of our heavenly Father, and it is frankly stupid. This is what pagans do; but it is an utterly unsuitable and unworthy ambition for Christians." We are not spiritual orphans. God loves and cares for us—He has all the resources of eternity at His hand for our disposal.

b) Staying in port

Alistair MacLean quotes a story from Tauler, the German mystic. One day Tauler met a poor man. "God give you a good day, my friend," he said. The poor man answered, "I thank God I never had a bad one." Then Tauler said, "God give you a happy life, my friend." "I thank God," said the poor man, "I am never unhappy." Tauler in amazement said, "What do you mean?" "Well," said the poor man, "when it is fine, I thank God; when it rains, I thank God; when I have plenty, I thank God; when I am hungry, I thank God; and since God's will is my will, and whatever pleases Him pleases me, why should I say I am unhappy when I am not?" Tauler looked at the man in astonishment. "Who are you?" he asked. "I am a king," said the poor man. "Where then is your kingdom?" asked Tauler. And the poor man answered quietly, "In my heart." Someone has said, "I am always happy, and my secret is always to sail the seas, and ever to keep the heart in port." Isaiah put it this way, "Thou wilt keep him in perfect peace, whose mind is stayed on thee, because he trusteth in thee" (Isa. 26:3). Now, how do you find this port?

III. THE GUARANTEED PROMISE (v. 33)

"But seek ye first the kingdom of God, and his righteousness, and all these things shall be added unto you."

In other words, get your thoughts on the divine level, and God will take care of the physical. God doesn't want us involved in the physical; He wants to free us from that.

A. The Contrast

"But."

According to Arndt and Gingrich's *Greek-English Lexicon*, the primary use of *de* ("but") is to emphasize a contrast. The best way to translate it is "rather." Rather than worrying, rather than being like the pagans, rather than being of little faith, rather than bringing the future into the present, "seek ye first the kingdom of God." Rather than seeking what the Gentiles seek, rather than being materialistically oriented, rather than being consumed with the possessions of this age, seek the kingdom.

B. The Concern

"Seek ye first."

The Greek word *prōtos* means "first in a line of more than one option." Of all the priorities of life, this is number one.

1. "The kingdom of God."

What does it mean to seek the kingdom? The kingdom is simply *basileia* in the Greek, meaning "Christ's rule, the rule of God, the reign of God, the dominion of God, the kingdom of God." We should seek that which is eternal. According to Matthew 6:10 we are to pray, "Thy kingdom come." We are to be lost in the kingdom of God.

The apostle Paul, on his way to Jerusalem and preaching the gospel of the kingdom, prepared to defend his faith at the point of a sword. The people kept saying, "Don't go, Paul. When you get there you are going to get in a lot of trouble. They are going to put you in prison, and they might take your life." So Paul said, "But none of these things move me, neither count I my life dear unto myself" (Acts 20:24*a*). He was not interested in adding a cubit to his life span; he was not concerned that he got enough to eat and wear. He continued "so that I might finish my course with joy, and the ministry, which I have received of the Lord Jesus" (Acts 20:24*b*).

This is the priority that will make someone go to a mission field in obscurity and say good-bye to all the fashions and fancy foods of the world—to eat and dress in a very simple way, isolating his whole life in that situation because he is not nearly so concerned about those things as he is with the advance of the kingdom. This is what makes someone preach Christ to the point where he doesn't even fear for his life because the kingdom is far beyond any other concern.

a) Conversion

Where is your heart and your preoccupation? Are you more concerned with the kingdom, or are you more concerned with this world? Are you pouring all of your energies into the globe, or are you investing yourself in God's eternal kingdom? Seeking the kingdom means you seek to bring people to Christ

95

because you seek the growth of the kingdom, you seek the gospel of the kingdom to be preached, and you seek for people to become redeemed. We do not spread the gospel because of some kind of a "sinful imperialism or triumphalism," as John Stott says. We do not seek to advance the kingdom for any selfish goals but for the glory of God.

b) Commitment

Seeking the kingdom also means that I seek Christ's rule to be manifest in my life. I seek the kingdom of God to be revealed in my life as righteousness, peace, and joy in the Holy Spirit (Rom. 14:17). So, when the world sees righteousness, peace, and joy in my life instead of worry, it knows the kingdom of God is there. You can say, "I want people to be saved, and I want to tell them all about Jesus." But if your life is marked by worry, anxiety, and concern, they will not believe you have anything they want. They are certainly going to question the power of God. The kingdom of God is manifest in righteousness, peace, and joy in the Holy Spirit—that overcomes the worry. So, we seek the kingdom when we seek to bring people into the kingdom and when we let it be manifest through us.

c) Coming again

Third, we seek the kingdom when we long for Jesus to return in His millennial glory. I can't get too excited about piling up stuff in this world because I am going to get it all for nothing when the kingdom comes. The Bible says that we will be joint heirs with Christ (Rom. 8:17), we will reign with Him forever and ever (Rev. 22:5), we will have a new heaven and a new earth throughout all eternity (Rev. 21:1), and we will have all of the majesty and the riches of eternal heaven (Rev. 21:1—22:5). Why should I waste all my time stockpiling this stuff when the whole earth is going to be destroyed and the Lord is going to make a new one?

So, seeking the kingdom is to seek that which is yet in the future—the granting of eternal glory that comes from Christ when He gives His saints His own kingdom. It is to see the kingdom manifest in my life through righteousness, peace, and joy. And it is to desire to win people to

Jesus so that the kingdom might grow and expand.

2. "And his righteousness"

Don't chase money; chase holiness—pursue it. He is talking about practical righteousness. When you pursue something, pursue godliness, holiness, and righteousness. Some of us spend all our time pursuing money, cars, houses, clothes, and so on. You say, "If I get involved in the kingdom and chasing holiness, then what happens?"

C. The Care

"And all these things shall be added unto you."

According to Psalm 84:11b, if you walk uprightly you will never have any need. God will take care of those who seek His kingdom and His righteousness.

Solomon provides for us an excellent illustration. He didn't pray for riches, for fancy clothes, for fancy food, and for a long life. He prayed for wisdom. When he received wisdom, he received all the rest. No one was ever dressed like Solomon, no one was ever as wealthy as Solomon, and no one put on feasts that could match his. The man was incredible—he sought wisdom, and in the getting of wisdom all the rest was residual.

If you worry, it is a sin—it is unnecessary because of your Father, it is uncharacteristic because of your faith, and it is unwise because of your future.

Focusing on the Facts

1. Why is it going to be difficult for Americans to maintain their current approach to life? Why do we presently have this particular approach (see p. 82)?
2. What is one possible solution to our present approach to life? What part do Christians have to play in this solution (see p. 82)?
3. What are the three reasons for investing our treasure in heaven (see pp. 83-84)?
4. What four characteristics of God should eliminate any need for anxiety on our part (see p. 85)?
5. Explain the argument that Jesus gives in Matthew 7:7-11. Why can we trust God to give us what we need (see p. 85)?
6. List some verses that show that God provides for His people (see pp. 86-87).
7. What things did Peter worry about? What lesson did he finally learn (see pp. 86-87)?

8. What kind of faith is manifested when someone worries (see p. 87)?

9. What is significant about the fact that each time Jesus used the phrase "O ye of little faith" He was speaking to the disciples (see p. 88)?

10. What are four results of worry? Explain what each means (see pp. 88-89).

11. What is the number one cause for people not trusting God (see p. 89)?

12. Who are the "Gentiles"? Why do they seek after the necessities of life (see p. 90)?

13. How do the people of the world view the deities they have created? What do their deities do for them? Who are their deities (see p. 90)?

14. What kind of mind-set is revealed in those who do not trust God? What is the proper mind-set? Support your answer (see pp. 90-91).

15. What is the basic difference between our God and the gods of the pagans (see p. 91)?

16. Why is lack of joy a sin? Why do people lack joy? Why shouldn't you worry about tomorrow (see p. 92)?

17. When is God's grace made available to believers? In light of this fact, why is it wrong to worry about tomorrow (see p. 93)?

18. What priority must we have, for God to take care of our physical needs (see p. 94)?

19. What is "the kingdom of God" (see p. 95)?

20. What three things are manifested in the lives of those who seek first after God's kingdom? Explain how each is manifested in the life of a believer (see pp. 95-96).

21. In what three ways should the kingdom of God be revealed in a believer's life (Rom. 14:17; see p. 96)?

Pondering the Principles

1. In their book, Jeremy Rifkin and Ted Howard call for a return to the Christian ethic of unselfishness and low consumption. A better word for unselfishness might be humility. Look up the following verses: Philippians 1:29—2:11; James 4:1-10; 1 Peter 5:5-10. Write down as many observations as you can on what these verses teach about humility. How are those who are not humble described? According to James 4:4, where do their loyalties lie? What is consistently a part of a humble Christian walk? What did Jesus Christ endure according to Philippians 2:8? Can a Christian live a humble life without experiencing suffering

(see Phil. 1:29; 1 Pet. 5:10)? What does God do for those who live a humble life? Where is Jesus Christ right now? According to 1 Peter 5:7, one part of humbling yourself under the mighty hand of God is that you will cast all your care on Him. Take the time to do that right now, and begin to live a life of humility, knowing that God will reward your commitment.

2. Do you possess little faith or much faith? Do you trust God in the situations you become anxious about? Does your life contradict the promises God has made to you in His Word? Are the circumstances in your life determining how you behave rather than the Word of God? Do you know God well? If not, how can you know Him better? Read Joshua 1:8. What are the results that God promises to one who will meditate on His Word day and night? Will you covenant with God to get to know Him by spending time in His Word daily?

3. Do you face life like a Christian or like a person who does not know God? When life is difficult and the future is insecure, how do you react? Does your Christian faith affect your view of life? How? Do you always place every trial, every anticipation of the future, and every present situation in the context of your faith? If you are not facing your life experiences as a Christian should, you need to make some changes in your life. Begin those changes with prayer. As an incentive to your prayer, memorize Philippians 4:6: "Be anxious for nothing, but in everything, by prayer and supplication with thanksgiving, let your requests be made known unto God."

4. The priority for a Christian, along with seeking God's kingdom, is also seeking His righteousness. Look up the following verses: Psalm 42:1; Matthew 5:6; John 6:35. With how much intensity should you seek after righteousness? How does this hunger and thirst for righteousness become fully satisfied? Read Romans 8:3-5; 2 Corinthians 3:18; and 2 Thessalonians 2:13. Spend time in prayer thanking God for having chosen you to salvation through sanctification in the Spirit. Based on this, begin to seek after God's kingdom and righteousness with a hunger and thirst that only God can satisfy.

Scripture Index

Genesis
3:19   70
22:14   52
45:22   34

Exodus
20:15,17   13
20:17   9

Leviticus
7:30-35   6

Deuteronomy
8:18   14
28   7
28:1-6   7-8
28:1-14   13
28:15-19   8

Joshua
7   11
7:21   34
14:8   40

Judges
14:12   34

1 Samuel
2   6
2:12-17   6

2 Kings
5:22   34

1 Chronicles
29:11   49
29:11-12   51

2 Chronicles
20:7   14

Nehemiah
8:1   26
8:5-6,8   26
9:38   26
10:32   27
10:33,35-39   27

Job
38:41   68
42:12   14

Psalms
16:8   40
24:1   49
34:10   86
37:25   53
84:11   97
89:33   32
138:8   32
147:9   68

Proverbs
3:9-10   31
6:6,8   15
10:22   9
11:24-25   31
14:23   15
19:17   33
21:20   15
22:7   15
23:4   9
23:6   38
23:7   28
24:3-4   15
28:19   15
28:20   9
28:22   38
30:8-9   18, 57

Ecclesiastes
1:2   9, 11

Isaiah
26:3   94

Lamentations
3:23   92

Daniel
2:20-21   52
6   52

Matthew
5:1—6:18   4-5

5-7	4
5:20	4, 25
6:10	95
7:7-11	85
8:24-26	87
13:44	35
14:29-31	86
14:31	87
16:8	87
16:22	87
19:21,29	12-13
19:24	7
21:12-13	6-7
25	14
27:5	11

Luke

6:38	31
12:15	54, 81
12:16-18	56
12:18	35
12:28	87
12:30	53, 90
12:33	33
16:9	33
16:11	37
16:14	9
19	14
19:2,9	14

John

2:13-17	6-7
3:16	32
4:14	32
6:27	28
6:37,39	32
17:15	91
18:10	87

Acts

1:18-19	11
2	30
2:45	30
5:1-11	11, 13-14
5:3-4	13
20:24	95

Romans

6:16-18	39
8:17	96
8:29-30	32
8:39	32
12:2	91
12:8	37
12:11	15
14:17	96

1 Corinthians

4:7	14
4:13	55
10:31	9

2 Corinthians

9:6	31
9:13	37
12:14	16

Ephesians

1:18-19	89

Philippians

4:6	91
4:11-12	48
4:19	52, 54, 55, 86

Colossians

3:5	17

2 Thessalonians

3:10	70

1 Timothy

3:3	56
5:8	16
6:8	53
6:10	10
6:17	14
6:17-19	32

2 Timothy

4:10	11

Hebrews

13:5	54
13:8	93

James

1:5	37

1 Peter

1:4	32

3:3-4	74	Revelation	
5:2	6	18	47
5:7	87	21:1—22:5	96

Moody Press, a ministry of the Moody Bible Institute, is designed for education, evangelization, and edification. If we may assist you in knowing more about Christ and the Christian life, please write us without obligation: Moody Press, c/o MLM, Chicago, Illinois 60610.